GRADUAL REFORMATION INTOLARABLE
By C. Matthew McMahon and Anthony Burgess

COPYRIGHT INFORMATION

Gradual Reformation Intolerable
By C. Matthew McMahon and Anthony Burgess

Edited by Therese B. McMahon

Copyright © 2011-2014 by Puritan Publications and A Puritan's Mind

Some language and grammar has been updated from the original manuscript. Any change in wording or punctuation has not changed the intent or meaning of the original author(s), and has been made to aid the modern reader.

Published by Puritan Publications
A Ministry of A Puritan's Mind
2633 Lantana Road
Crossville, TN 38572
www.puritanpublications.com
www.apuritansmind.com

All rights reserved. No part of this publication may be reproduced, stored in a retrieval system or transmitted in any form by any means, electronic, mechanical, photocopy, recording or otherwise, without the prior permission of the publisher, except as provided by USA copyright law.

This Second Edition, 2014
Manufactured in the United States of America

ISBN: 978-1-62663-107-6
eISBN: 978-1-62663-108-3

TABLE OF CONTENTS

GRADUAL REFORMATION INTOLARABLE............1
COPYRIGHT INFORMATION 2
TABLE OF CONTENTS.......................................3

PART 1

GRADUAL REFORMATION INTOLERABLE...............5
MARTIN LUTHER AND TRUE BIBLICAL REFORMATION... 22
JOHN CALVIN AND TRUE BIBLICAL REFORMATION... 29
REGULATING LIFE BY GOD'S PRINCIPLES............ 34

PART 2

MEET ANTHONY BURGESS... 48
ORIGINAL TITLE PAGE... 54
APPOINTMENT 55
TO THE HONORABLE HOUSE OF COMMONS NOW ASSEMBLED IN PARLIAMENT..........................56
A SERMON FOR THE HONORABLE HOUSE OF COMMONS AT THE PUBLIC FAST SEPTEMBER 27, 1643 59

Table of Contents

THE TEXT OPENED 59
THE DOCTRINE 62
CAUTIONS 71
FAITH 74
WORSHIP AND DISCIPLINE 75
LIVING HOLY 76
USE 1. OF EXHORTATION TO SET UP THIS RULE.
.... 78
CONSEQUENCES 85
THREE THINGS WHICH ARE NECESSARY 92
THE TESTIMONY ITSELF 94
HINDRANCES TO REFORM 96
MOTIVES TO PURSUE REFORMATION 103
USE OF EXHORTATION 107
AN INSTRUCTION ON VERSE 2 112

GRADUAL REFORMATION INTOLERABLE

By C. Matthew McMahon, Ph.D., Th.D.

Leviticus 26:23-24, "And if by these things you are not *reformed* by Me, but walk contrary to Me, then I also will walk contrary to you, and I will punish you yet seven times for your sins."

The purpose of this double work is to set forth the nature of *true biblical reformation*.[1] Christians will often pick up books on "*the* Reformation" hoping to read about William Tyndale, Martin Luther or John Calvin. One cannot mention "*the* Reformation" without mentioning those names. Such books usually center on the hammering of Luther's 95 *Theses* on the door of the Wittenberg Church in 1517, and from there they begin to tell the story of how God providentially brought about spiritual revival for the good of His church. But this book is not historical *perse*, rather, it is theologically practical. It is designed to take the

---

[1] See my larger treatment of each sphere of work to promote Reformation in "A Heart for Reformation."

biblical principles of reformation, which were the practical out workings of the theology behind the Word of God, and apply them to the contemporary church. Is this simply preaching? No. It is a combined effort to first distinguish true reformation as the Bible explains and then allow Burgess in the second half of the work to press it into our conscience in puritan style. This is the aim of both my section of this book and of Burgess' treatment of the difficulties encountered when Reformation *begins*.

I have said this many times and in many contexts: it is impossible to document history simply as chronological events, but rather it is the *intrusion* of God into time to establish His *redemptive* purposes in and through men, and declare His person and glory through the work of Jesus Christ. Two epochs in God's work point to the greatest revolutions and revivals ever documented: the entrance of the Lord of Glory in the fullness of time in the little town of Bethlehem, and the era of the Reformation breaking out of a reign of eclipsing doctrinal darkness and superstition. Christ brought forth the Gospel of Jesus Christ, and the Reformers rescued the Gospel from drowning in a sea of ecclesiastical expedience. But what should

Christians think concerning revival *today*? Is there room in the present day for *further* "reformation"?

"Reformation" is defined by *Webster's Dictionary* as "a 16th century religious movement marked ultimately by rejection or modification of some Roman Catholic doctrine and practice and establishment of the Protestant churches." That is the *historical* definition. There is another: "Reformation is the state of being "reformed." Now one has to ask, from a biblical perspective, what this means. To be "reformed" or to "reform" means, "1a) to put or change into an improved form or condition 1b) to amend or improve by change of form or removal of faults or abuses 2) to put an end to an evil by enforcing or introducing a better method or course of action, 3) to induce or cause to abandon evil ways." Reformation, then, confronts and changes the *status quo* in order to improve, amend, and introduce a better method of procedure. It removes, puts an end to, and abandons false or evil ways that hinder that which should already be in place. In terms of *the* Reformation, it is the abandonment and repudiation of the evil or wicked devices of men instituted in the church through false doctrines, and to establish, change, and amend those ways by immediate interposition of improved change to the foundations of ecclesiastical truth found in Scripture. Such a term as "reformed", then, has some very important biblical connotations as well as historical connotations that must be embraced. The importance here is a formal *return* to sound doctrine and truth previously eclipsed, and put into sanctifying *action*.

John Calvin poured many hours into writing various polemical works for the church that described and outlined how reformation should take place under varying circumstances. One of these works is called, *The Necessity of Reforming the Church*. It answers the following inquiry, "The question is not, whether the Church labors under diseases both numerous and grievous, (this is admitted even by all moderate judges,) but whether the diseases are of a kind the cure of which admits not of longer delay, and as to which, therefore, it is neither useful nor becoming to await the result of slow remedies. We are accused of rash and impious innovation, for having ventured to propose any change at all on the former state of the Church." Calvin wrote this tract while a Diet (a council) was taking place in the city of Spires, and desired to present it at the Diet in hopes of *further* reformation. The work covers three aspects of Reformation, 1) the evils which compelled the reformers to seek for remedies; 2) That the particular remedies which the Reformers employed were apt and salutary; and 3) That the reformers were not at liberty any longer to delay putting forth our hand, in as much as the matter demanded instant amendment. Calvin and the other Swiss reformers had been branded as working too *quickly* for Reformation. But Calvin replies in saying that they had not done anything too hastily, or rashly, desiring to show the necessity of their reforms over and against the intolerableness of a gradual reformation. Theodore Beza, one of Calvin's lifelong friends at Reformation, says of the work, "I know not if any writing on the subject, more nervous or solid, has been published in our age."

    The matters which Calvin disputed in this tract on reforming the Church are 1) the cloak of evil hiding the head doctrines of the Christian faith, 2) the neglect of the pure worship of God, 3) the sacraments being polluted and administered amiss, and 4) the government of the church being corrupted by "insufferable tyranny." The biblical foundations of Christianity are overthrown when these areas of sacred doctrine are neglected, overshadowed or compromised. In reaction to this, actual reformation needed to take place, and even in this present day still must take place. It would do the church well to have 1) theologians who rightly know the Word in such a way as to stand upon it in the face of any other unorthodox views that attempt to corrupt the true doctrines of the faith, 2) pastors who are well equipped to train and teach these doctrines to the church, and 3) laymen who are willing to receive such teaching in the face of popular Christianity. If the areas of higher education were theologically sound, and that education transferred both theologically and practically to pastors who desire to teach the people of God the Word of God, and the people of God desired to hold to such sound doctrine and practical teaching, the church would be a far different place than it is today as a whole. If Calvin were alive today, he would have to write the same tract again, but with a more pressing angle since the church so easily is swayed by every wind of doctrine, and every popular level of Evangelicalism.

    The subtitle of Calvin's polemic is, *Seriously To Undertake The Task Of Restoring The Church*, and it is dedicated, "In The Name Of All Who Wish Christ To

Reign." Calvin desired to repair the improper worship of God, and bring the church back to a pure worship that honors Christ. Calvin was not willing to simply "undertake" reformation, but "seriously to undertake the task" of restoring the biblical Gospel to the worship and life of the Church. The Scriptural rule of worship should be followed as accurately as it is stated and exemplified in the Word of God. This rule, or principle, distinguishes between pure worship that is of universal application by God's command, and human folly that changes worship into "will-worship," or the worship of "the self" instead of God. "We should," as Calvin says, "strictly enjoin what he wishes us to do," as well as "at once" reject every human invention that does not line up with the Word of God. Calvin presses the immediate need for reformation in worship that does not strictly adhere to the commandment of the Word. But he did not stop there. In adhering to the regulative principles found in the Word of God, these principles not only regulate the worship of the church, but also extend or are annexed to "all the actions of our lives." This meant that the church was only one sphere in which reform should take place. True biblical Reformation will affect every area of the Christian life.

It will affect the Church, the Home, Society, places of employment, in a word – everywhere. The practical outworking of following the Regulative Principle is its extensions in a right ordering of life in general after the Word of God. But this cannot happen without having a right heart for Reformation.

Those who have a heart after true biblical Reformation will ultimately see a change in the manner that the Christian religion brings them *coram deo*, before the face of God. Such a Reformation, through the true Gospel of Jesus Christ and justification by faith alone, will unite Christians to God in a more intimate manner than what pop Christianity can offer on some emotional high. Such pop Christianity is not true biblical Christianity. Today, smorgasbord niceties are packaged within the term "Evangelicalism." But current Evangelicalism is not the same as it was during the time of the Reformation, or of any time of "reformation" through the history of the biblical narratives of God's people. During the Reformation, the term "Evangelical" was used to describe the reformers who believed in "gospelling" or heralding the good news of justification by faith alone. In contrast to the Roman Catholic Church of the day, Protestants were known as these

"Evangelicals." Those in league with Wittenberg and the Swiss cantons toward Reformation were frequently referred to as Evangelical by the Roman Church. Reformation doctrine, then, historically, was associated with the term "reformed". And in those days "reformed" meant something very specific. However, today, this is not the case. Evangelicalism does not press for *reformation* any longer. They are more interested in theology dispensed by "Christian cartoons" or popular TV and radio preachers. In general the term "Evangelical" has developed into a more inclusivistic attitude toward liberalism, and is ecumenical in its worldwide efforts towards "ecclesiastical unity". As a result of a broad churchism this non-theological view is akin to simply pleasing the masses.

The Evangelical sector is made up of pastors, theologians and teachers who are best described as "theologically flexible." This is an oversimplification for many of them. This ecumenical and theological flexibility is a key factor (and problem) among contemporary Evangelicals. They are often noncompulsory and convicting in their preaching, and desire to keep "peace" in their churches for the sake of ecumenicalism. The problem that is faced is their flagrant inability to draw solid nonnegotiable doctrinal lines in the sand. And solid nonnegotiable doctrinal lines are what sparked every reformation from those accounted in the biblical narratives, to those that surrounded the Reformation of the 16th century, to the post-Reformation dogmatics that emerged as a result of fine tuning theology accomplish by English Puritanism during the 17th century, and the Great Awakenings later in the histories of England and America. In other words, to have reformation, one needs sound doctrine. But it is unfortunate that the church must look *back* in history to find those great old-aged redwood theologians. Why is it that they cannot look in their own churches?

When Christian book catalogues come to this writer's door, it is always interesting to find out what current Evangelicals think are the "best" books, or what books are "top sellers." In the latest catalogue to come by (a January / March Winter Catalogue), it housed 64 pages, of which only two had room for any books that were worthwhile, or even close to begin "biblically accurate." When opening up the catalogue, it begins with their "top sellers." Now in perusing these top sellers, what is listed? Rick Warren's "Purpose

Driven Life," and directly beneath that is his "Purpose Driven Church." Under that is found Max Lucado's "Come Thirsty", and just to the right is found "Your Best Life Now" by Joel Osteen. Just to the right of that, in a final column, is Joyce Meyers's two latest books, "Approval Addiction: Overcoming Your Need to Please Everyone," and "Battlefield of the Mind – updated Edition (as if another is needed). Yes, Benny Hinn is there too with some of his works, and charismaniacs adorn the rest of this section. With "top sellers" like these books written by *theological morons* and false teachers, one does not have to wonder too long why the American church is dying! What the church needs to do is stop worrying about the dollar and how much money one can make by selling theological drivel, and begin caring about what actually pleases God. Certainly, with nonsense like these books, and their watered down version of the Gospel (and certainly contrary versions of the Gospel), hitting the Christian marketplace, and making them top sellers, the church is 1) ignorant of the truth, and 2) in desperate need of a *thorough* reformation that is Christ-glorifying.

Reformation is always something that is accomplished *thoroughly* as well. Again, be reminded, historically speaking, being *reformed* meant something *specific*. It should be agreed that being "Reformed" or going about "Reformation" meant something to Ulrich Zwingli, William Tyndale, Martin Luther, John Calvin and other reformers. History, though, gives way to how it is accomplished practically. It is not something that men are allowed to take in "part" in the name of "reforming" or simply to be associated with that which is "reformed". Men ought not say they are all for "true biblical reformation" if they could not, in good conscience, claim the entirety of the Reformed faith if they simply believed one tenth of what the Reformation taught, or what the Bible teaches about true biblical Reformation. Also, they could not, in good conscience call themselves Reformed or claim the Reformed faith if they simply believed nine tenths of what the Reformation taught, and rejected the other one tenth completely. They must, of necessity, embrace Reformation doctrine to claim the Reformed banner. In like manner they cannot believe four points of the five points of Calvinism and call themselves a Calvinist. Those who believe the doctrines of grace know this little ploy used too well by confused Arminians who say such things. But the orthodox know such doctrinal deviation is wrong, or at the very least, they know that such people are extremely confused. It is much the same with the doctrines of the Reformation, and what the bible teaches about true biblical reformation. One cannot reject Reformed worship, those foundational guidelines within the orthodox realm of Reformed doctrine, and say they are Reformed. They cannot discard church discipline and say they are Reformed. They cannot reject key aspects of Covenant Theology and call themselves Reformed. They cannot misuse the sacraments, or deny them, and call themselves Reformed. Holding to certain biblical ideologies determines whether one is Reformed or not. What do the Scriptures say?

Leviticus 26:23-24, "And if by these things you are not *reformed* by Me, but walk contrary to Me, then I also will walk contrary to you, and I will punish you yet seven times for your sins."

Hebrews 9:9-10, "It was symbolic for the present time in which both gifts and sacrifices are offered which cannot make him who performed the service perfect in regard to the conscience concerned only with foods and drinks, various washings, and fleshly ordinances imposed until the time of *reformation*."

Gradual Reformation Intolerable

I would like to remind the reader how true biblical reformation played out in the history of the Reformation, and the nature or course that reformation took under the guidance of able men such as Luther and Calvin. By comparing the nature of true biblical reformation in action, individual reformation in like manner may come to pass more readily. The reader should beware – gradual reformation is always *intolerable* to those who love the Word of God, and strive to uphold that Word in the life of the church, family and individual before Jesus Christ. In this way, is a gradual reformation intolerable to you?

The European Reformation embodies the biblical guide to the nature of true reform and the convictions needful towards an authentic transformation of a corrupt church into a holy body. This will be proven in a moment. The notion, then, of a gradual Reformation is at best *intolerable*. The saints of God should never settle for a "gradual reformation." Josiah, when confronted with the Law of God made radical changes in the *cultus* of Israel. In like manner, Martin Luther and John Calvin vigorously contended for the Reformation of the church, not a gradual accommodation in hopes of reform. It is true that the

Reformers did not desire schism from the corrupt church. Rather, they desired to instill truth into it and recapture the virtue that had been lost under a cloak of spiritual degeneracy. Yet, after true biblical reformation had begun, the Roman Catholic Church could not accept such changes. The reformers knew that such changes would ultimately force the Protestants to break from the Roman Catholic Church in order to reestablish the virtues of biblical Christianity. In this way, it is impossible to deny that after the biblical Gospel settled in the hands of converted reformers, pastors and theologians of that day (as in previous biblical days) that true Reformation progressed through impositions upon certain immediate and necessary obligations in relation to ecclesiology (the regulative principle of worship and church discipline) and Sacramentology (the right administration of the sacraments). In other words, the nature of worship is not something that the church should gradually work its way into. Rather, as God has so commanded His people, they should obey. It is the same as with lying. If a man is a compulsive liar, should he gradually change or should be repent of his lying? Would it be acceptable to God to lie a little, and gradually change, or does require men to repent of their sin?

In the 2007 movie "Amazing Grace", William Wilberforce is shown over his 15 year attempt at abolishing slavery in England. The slave trade had grown so wicked, that freighting ships would take on more salves in their hulls than they were allowed by double the amount, and over 600 of 800 slaves would die on the journey home. While recounting all the horrific statistics of these trade ships, Wilberforce attempted time and time again over that 15 year span, to have Parliament abolish slavery. One man, teetering on a dubious middle position, stood up and agreed with Wilberforce that slavery should be abolished, but only gradually. How does one take into account the atrocities of the slave trade and desire to "gradually" put an end to it? In the same way and manner God is not pleased with a "gradual reformation" of the essential truths of the bible, but a thorough reform like the one Josiah enacted in his day.

Gradual reformation has never been the matrix in which the church has functioned since its inception in the Garden of Eden. Yet, various New Testament epistles embrace a tenderness in which reformation should be accomplished, and in some instances, elementary doctrines should be taught again (*e.g.* Hebrews 5:12-14). It is a tragedy that churches, at various points in their spirituality, cannot bear to hear certain doctrines or ideas lest they become overwhelmed because of their inadequacy in understanding the Bible. Nonetheless, in beginning to teach elementary doctrines again, this does not infer that the foundations of basic principles be abandoned in order to accommodate the people of God in their waywardness. It is the opinion of the reformers that a context for teaching biblically sound doctrine is only found in a church that desires to lay the principles of a biblical reformation down first, and then advance in biblical teaching from those basic fundamental maxims.

Let us recap the basic definition of what it means to reform something. Just a moment ago "Reformation" was defined as "a 16th century *religious movement* marked ultimately by *rejection* or *modification* of some Roman Catholic doctrine and practice and establishment of the Protestant churches."[2] It is the state of being "reformed." To be "reformed" or to "reform" means, "1a) to put or change into an improved

---

[2] Emphasis mine.

form or condition 1b) to amend or improve by change of form or removal of faults or abuses 2) *to put an end to an evil by enforcing or introducing a better method or course of action*, 3) to induce or *cause to abandon* evil ways."[3] In terms of *the* Reformation, it is the abandonment and repudiation of evil or wicked devices of men instituted in the church through false doctrines, and to establish, change and amend those ways by immediate interposition of improved change to the foundations of ecclesiastical truth found in Scripture. That is a mouthful! In simpler terminology - it is a formal return to sound doctrine and truth previously eclipsed by sin and ignorance – and it was not accomplished gradually.

MARTIN LUTHER AND TRUE BIBLICAL REFORMATION

In considering the biblical actions of Martin Luther in Germany, we find an instantaneous imposition of reform once Luther embraces the truth of the Word of God. Luther was converted, became a priest, went to Rome, and upon his return within 2 years, set the 95 *Theses* in motion. Yet, even before this,

---

[3] Emphasis mine.

being a learned Doctor of Theology, his fame was spreading through Europe attracting students from every nearby country. Scholastic philosophy and theological methods had been undermined, and a *via moderna* (a new and modern way) of yet another sort stood in its place. Just as Jesus began his public ministry with the expulsion of the profane traffickers from the court of the temple (John 2:14ff), so Luther began his ministry by preaching and lecturing *against* relics and indulgences – a desire to rid the Roman Church of its abuses against the people of God. The official statement to this did not come long afterwards, but relatively quickly in the *95 Theses*.

The Reformation began with a public protest against the traffic of indulgences that profaned and degraded the Christian religion.[4] Phillip Schaff writes, "After serious deliberation, without consulting any of his colleagues or friends, but following an irresistible impulse, Luther resolved upon a public act of unforeseen consequences."[5] Luther's desire was not to break off from the church under these reforms, but to

---

[4] Phillip Schaff, *History of the Christian Church*, Volume 7, Grand Rapids, MI, 1994. Page 118.
[5] Martin Luther's *95 Thesis*, Ages Software, 2000.

debate in the accepted manner of scholasticism on the questions raised by his *95 Theses* against indulgences. At first, Pope Leo X did not bother with the *Theses* believing it was simply the ravings of a drunken monk whose influence would soon dissipate. But when Luther's "reforms" began to reach into the pocket of the Pope, Leo wanted him silenced. The fact that such a document was made public, and pinned on a church door, attests that this crucial move was not one done in secret. There were no pretenses in Luther's actions at all. Reformation makes men bold in God's power and grace.

What was Luther's response to Rome's desire for him to stop preaching the truth after the *Theses* was published? With the "stroke of an axe" the Reformation began, but was there a lapse in its continuation? Luther's mind was bound to the Word of God and unless one could convince him of his errors by its authority, he would not change his course. Even the *Theses* read, "I implore all men, by the faith of Christ, either to point out to me a better way, if such a way has been divinely revealed to any, or at least to submit their opinion to the judgment of God and of the Church."[6] In attempting to silence Luther, Pope Leo had Prierias write a "crushing blow" against the *Theses* in Latin. Luther replied, and then Prierias replied back again. The correspondence simply widened the breach already begun by Luther. Yet, even while this correspondence was occurring, Rome had already decided to brand Luther as a heretic, and commanded him to appear in Rome within sixty days to recant his heresies. Luther met with the cordial Cajetan three times. Cajetan attempted to dissuade Luther, through a cordial friendship, and demanded of him strict allegiance to the Pope and a retraction of his errors. Upon his last meeting, Cajetan threatened him with excommunication having already the papal mandate in his hand, and dismissed him with the words, "Revoke, or do not come again into my presence."[7] Luther did not bend. Rather, he escaped that night and rode back to Wittenberg. Is this the ploy of *gradual* Reformation?

Before being called to the Diet of Worms, another attempt was made to silence Luther when Pope Leo sent Karl von Miltitz to meet with him in

---

[6] Phillip Schaff, *History of the Christian Church*, Volume 7, Grand Rapids, MI, 1994. Page 32.
[7] Schaff, 35.

order to, affably, aid him in recanting his heresy. After the meeting, Miltitz seemed to believe he made headway with Luther, yet Luther would not think of recanting his ideas. Luther did write a humble letter to the Pope expressing his desire to reform the church, but not to recant his ideas. At the same time, Pope Leo had a papal bull drawn up which demanded his recantation, or his excommunication and death. Luther's response to this was a public gathering of students and faculty at Wittenberg to witness the burning of the papal bull, upon reception of it. The implementations of these acts do not lend itself to a gradual reformation, but a Reformation that imposed restriction and reaction against false doctrine. In no way, and at no time, could Luther go back to the false doctrine that he had been raised upon as a monk just to appease the consciences of men. Gradual Reformation in any way is intolerable to the truth, as it was to Luther who stood upon the Word. The doctrines of grace and justification were planted in the heart of the Reformer and could not be removed. *Reformation* was based on these *convictions* brought about *by the Word of God*. Miller says, "Henceforth the doctrine of justification by faith alone was for him to the end of life the sum and substance of the gospel, the heart of theology, the central truth of Christianity, the article of the standing or falling church."[8]

Knowing Luther had not yet recanted, a Diet was called by Charles V (where Pope Leo X was represented) where Luther was summoned to Wittenberg. He was asked two questions in which he would reply in German and Latin – 1) Are these your writings? and, 2) Will you recant them? Luther asked for time in which to gather his thoughts and give a reply. Some would say this desire is exemplary of a "gradual reformation," however, the night was spent in prayer in order to answer them in a manner in which would be glorifying to God.[9] Luther had no intentions of recanting. Schaff says, "On the same evening Luther recollected himself, and wrote to a friend: I shall not retract one iota, so Christ help me."[10] Upon the next day these questions were placed on him again. His answer is the epitome of a rejection of gradual reformation, "Unless I am refuted and convicted by testimonies of the Scriptures or by clear arguments (since I believe neither the Pope nor the Councils alone;

---

[8] Arthur Miller, *Miller's Church History*, (Ages software, 2000), 104.
[9] See d'Aubigne's *History of the Reformation in the 16th Century* for Luther's prayer that night.
[10] Schaff, 53.

it being evident that they have often erred and contradicted themselves), I am conquered by the Holy Scriptures quoted by me, and my conscience is bound to the word of God: I can not and will not recant any thing, since it is unsafe and dangerous to do any thing against the conscience." If Luther really desired to "win their affections" and appease their consciences, he could have thrown aside the Scriptures and simply bowed down to Emperor Charles V. Instead his recapitulation of Christ's words, "If I have spoken evil, bear witness of me," testifies to his solidity toward reforming the church through the washing of the Word of God.

After the doctrinal break made with Rome the German Reformation could not be stopped. It was excessive in terms of those "being reformed" but its excessive character is not surprising. Staupitz, Luther's father of monkery, held fast to the unity of the Roman Catholic Church and was intimidated and repelled by the *excesses* of the Reformation.[11] The Pope issued a papal bull against Luther. Delegates were sent to him in order to silence him. His former mentors were encouraged to dissuade him. John Eck, the renowned

---

[11] Schaff, 102.

Roman Catholic theologian debated his "heresies." A Diet led by the Emperor called him to recant. In all this Luther remained steadfast upon the Word of God. At this point, the Reformation for Luther did not slow down, but *increased*. It went *faster*. He debated the Swiss reformer Ulrich Zwingli on the meaning and sacramentology of the Lord's Supper, completed a New Testament translation in German, wrote vehemently against the abuses of the Roman Catholic Church, and wrote voluminously for the edification of the Protestant Church. Luther's Reformation was anything but gradual. Many of his reforms were reactionary and instilled overnight. It is historically impossible to call the reforms of the German church throughout Luther's day anything but "excessive," and the opposite of a "gradual and subtle Reformation." In this way, the reader must come to grips in noticing the same movements that Luther made mimicked the work of Josiah in the days of Israel. Reformation is according to the Word of God, complete and covenanted by oath to the truth of the Word.

JOHN CALVIN AND TRUE BIBLICAL REFORMATION

In the Swiss Reformation the writings of John Calvin are preeminent, and the work of Calvin in his tract *The Necessity of Reforming the Church* is the best treatment explaining his rejection of a gradual reformation over an actual *true biblical Reformation*. His work is readily accessible, and clearly articulates the grievances of overthrowing or hindering an actual Reformation from taking place.

Calvin's work in Geneva is exemplary of true biblical Reformation. Certainly there were extremes that should be avoided (such as the State's physical persecution of the Anabaptists, the consent to the burning of Servetus, and the abusive imprisonments against the Genevans themselves). Yet, even in avoiding the extremes, the Genevan model of Reformation coincides with the same foundation as the German Reformation did for Luther –once the Word of God is implemented, true biblical change (reformation) is inevitable. Calvin wanted to see *true* biblical reform take place so that the Regulative Principle of the Church would not be displaced. This was not something he wanted to see *gradually* take place over a period of fifty years, but something, based on the Word of God, that should take place *right now*.

Why is Calvin so adamant to press immediate reform instead of gradual reform? Every area of worship that is overthrown by the devices of men becomes void of worship to God's holy commandments. For instance, the Lord's Supper had been violently corrupted by the mass in Calvin's day, and turned into a "theatrical exhibition."[12] It was resembled more by magical arts (*sacerdotalism*), rather than testifying to the significance and truth of the Supper. It ceased to be worship, and became an exercise in futility – much like the estranged view of Zwingli's memorialism in his view of the Lord's Supper.

What are the remedies to overthrow sin within the church? According to Calvin, there must be an *immediate* return to the legitimate worship of God and the ground of salvation. In Calvin's day this would mean the expulsion of everything in "worship" not prescribed in the Bible by good and necessary inference or by the direct institution of God – no idolatry, prayers to the saints, transubstantiation, vestments, and the like. The Word of God should regulate worship, the sacraments were to be administered

---

[12] Calvin, *The Necessity of Reforming the Church*, 29.

rightly, and the government of the church should be set in order.

After setting forth the evils and the remedies to those evils concerning false worship, Calvin then pleads for "Reformation required without delay."[13] Though many would have desired to see Calvin silenced on these issues since they were creating a tumultuous season for the church, Calvin defends himself by demonstrating that such a peace devoid of reform is really a false peace, and a cloak that covers evil. And to rail against Calvin and the other reformers such as Luther (whom Calvin mentions in the work), is really to rail against God himself since these reformers were simply following the Scriptures and the warrants set therein. Calvin says, "In a corruption of sound doctrine so extreme, in a pollution of the sacraments so nefarious, in a condition of the Church so deplorable, those who maintain that we ought not to have felt so strongly, would have been satisfied with nothing less than a perfidious tolerance, by which we should have betrayed the worship of God, the glory of Christ, the salvation of men, the entire administration of the sacraments, and the government of the Church. There

---

[13] Calvin, 88.

is something specious in the name of moderation, and tolerance is a quality which has a fair appearance, and seems worthy of praise; but the rule which we must observe at all hazards is, never to endure patiently that the sacred name of God should be assailed with impious blasphemy — that his eternal truth should be suppressed by the devil's lies — that Christ should be insulted, his holy mysteries polluted, unhappy souls cruelly murdered, and the Church left to writhe in extremity under the effect of a deadly wound. This would be not meekness, but indifference about things to which all others ought to be postponed."[14] Such deceitful and disloyalty to the Word of God, and subsequently God himself, cannot be tolerated. Exacting the rightful administration of church discipline upon matters that deviate from the Word of God is most necessary. To have right worship prescribed by the Word, a right administration of the sacraments, and a right exercise of church discipline, are, as this tract vividly portrays, the marks of a *true* church.

In demonstrating the intentions behind Calvin's Genevan reforms and the necessity of their

---

[14] Calvin, 107-108.

instantaneous administration, as well as seeing, by example, the actions of Martin Luther filled with doctrinal zeal, can Christians imitate these men on sure ground that they acted biblically? Christian practices should consistently be guided by the principles of the Word of God. Is there evidence in the Word of God for laying an immediate foundation of biblical principles in the church as opposed to a long gradual reform? Did Luther and Calvin follow the *Bible* on this? To answer this question the following biblical texts speak to the issue: Lev. 10:3; 1 Samuel 15:22, Matthew 15:9, Col. 2:23; 2 Chron. 14:4 (cf. 1 Kings 15:3); 2 Chron. 29:1; 2 Kings 22:1ff; John 2:12ff.

REGULATING LIFE BY GOD'S PRINCIPLES

Lev. 10:3, 1 Samuel 15:22 and Matthew 15:9 set the standard and basis for the Regulative Principle of worship defined by Calvin above. Calvin goes to great lengths to prove this. Luther contested for the Word in this manner and the direction of the Word in every area of the church – which is why the Pope, Cardinals, and theologians of the Catholic Church were so irate with him (he placed the Word above everything and subsequently removed their power). Leviticus 10:3 demonstrates the sanctity of God's mind in worship, "And Moses said to Aaron, "This is what the LORD spoke, saying: 'By those who come near Me I must be regarded as holy; And before all the people I must be glorified.' "So Aaron held his peace." Here we see that the worshipper will sanctify the Lord in his worship to Him, or God will sanctify Himself in judgment against the worshipper (as Nadab and Abihu had been killed by God for offering strange fire). 1 Samuel 15:22 says, "Then Samuel said: "Has the LORD as great delight in burnt offerings and sacrifices, as in obeying the voice of the LORD? Behold, to obey is better than sacrifice, And to heed than the fat of rams." In this instance Saul had taken it upon himself to do what he wanted in worshipping God without the sanction of God or the help of Samuel, and so the rebuke is given – God disdains self-imposed worship offered up by selfish hearts. And Matthew 15:9 states, "And in vain they worship Me, Teaching as doctrines the commandments of men." Here the Lord Jesus explains that men will replace the true worship of the church with that which is expedient or satisfying for themselves. Jesus teaches that such worship leads to vanity, *i.e.* it is waste of time, and brings condemnation. God must be sanctified in worship (set apart and regarded as holy, honored with a right heart and right sacrifices, and worshipped in the context of His prescriptions of worship) not the vain self-flattery of a man made will worship.

Calvin spent a great amount of time working through Colossians 2:23a, "Which things have indeed a shew of wisdom in will worship..." To remind the reader, "will worship" is that which is fabricated and implemented in the stead of true worship. It is devised by men, and hinders communion with God. It may have a show of wisdom (*i.e.* people participating in it may think it is quite good and helpful) but in the end it simply tears people away from Christ and leads them astray. It is false worship, and causes a rift between the worshipper and the Lord. Experience does not dictate worship, or the forms of worship. Rather, the Word of God is the only rule by which worship is defined by what God commands and sanctions. Any attempt at addition or subtraction to His Word is done at the peril of men's souls.

Luther's mind was set ablaze when he understood the grace of God. He could not contain himself. He was thrust forth over a series of providences that pressed him ever forward towards the Reformation of the church. Calvin's defense of his actions, or all the actions of the Reformers, is based on the urgency of adhering to the Scriptural warrants for worship. If anything else is substituted or taken away, then true worship cannot be obtained. In this respect, the question must be asked of today's theologians, pastors and laymen, "Do the Scriptures warrant an *immediate* change or a gradual change in the Reformation of the church?" Calvin and Luther opted for an *immediate* change. Though the Scriptures command reform, and constitute that which is right for worship, do they also demonstrate the time in which reformation should take place? The answer is a resounding "yes." The Old Testament and the New Testament abound with examples of instant reform in the church bringing the people back to a right worship of God.

Most of the kings of Israel and Judah (God's "anointed" leaders) did *not* follow His Word. They implemented false worship to foreign gods for personal or national expediency. Some kings brought the people back to biblical worship. Time could be spent with the partial reform of Asa (though partial reform, even if it is enacted immediately, is never ultimately beneficial. (*cf.* 2 Chronicles 14:4)). Better lessons can be gleaned from the complete reforms of Hezekiah and obviously good king Josiah.

Hezekiah and Josiah demonstrated an *immediate* and *complete* reform over degenerated worship. Concerning Hezekiah, 2 Chronicles 29:2-3 says, "And he did that which was right in the sight of the LORD, according to all that David his father had done. He in the first year of his reign, in the first month, opened the doors of the house of the LORD, and repaired them." He continued to restore true worship, which would degenerate after his death in the reign of Manasseh, one of the most wicked and ruthless kings of Israel. In verses 35-36 it says, "So the service of the house of the LORD was set in order. And Hezekiah rejoiced, and all the people, that God had prepared the people: for the thing was done suddenly." The Hebrew word *pithowm* for "done suddenly" means "suddenly or surprisingly." This cleansing of the temple and restoration of true worship was done "at once." It was "unexpected" by the people, so to speak. It is clear that Hezekiah had the complete restoration of worship in mind, not by gradual means, but with immediacy, and according to the Word of God.

Josiah was no different. Josiah's account in the Biblical record gleams with *fervency* in his restoration and reformation of worship. Israel's history here mirrors the darkness of the Roman Catholic reign and the rise of the Reformers. Manasseh and Amon had plunged the people into false worship, again. They were burning their children in the hands of Molech, and worshipping on the high places. Manasseh has the longest reign of any king, and he was the most wicked of them all. During his reign Baal was a household name. Amon was as wicked as Manasseh, his father, and the people of God continued to have a famine from the truth of the Word. Under their reigns, the Law of God was lost. After the death of Amon, Josiah rose to the throne and began to reign at 8 years old. Once he attained a mature age (eighteen) he reigned powerfully. He began a restoration of worship even before he had received the book of the Law that would have been discovered some 7 years later. After finding and reading the Law, 2 Kings 23:3-4 records the following, "And the king stood by a pillar, and made a covenant before the LORD, to walk after the LORD, and to keep his commandments and his testimonies and his statutes with all their heart and all their soul, to perform the words of this covenant that were written in this book. And all the people stood to the covenant. And the king commanded Hilkiah the high priest, and the priests of the second order, and the keepers of the door, to bring forth out of the temple of the LORD all the vessels that were made for Baal, and for the grove, and for all the host of heaven: and he burned them without Jerusalem in the fields of Kidron, and carried the ashes of them unto Bethel." The King had torn his robes and reinstated worship based on the book of the Law. He wasted no time and immediately restored the worship of God. He burned everything that desecrated the house of the Lord down at the river Kidron, and killed all the idolatrous priests who offered up worship to false gods. He crushed the statues of Molech, burned the chariots of the Sun, smashed every graven image into dust and destroyed all the altars that Ahaz had set up years earlier. He even burned the bones of dead men in the sepulchers because the people were worshipping them. Then, 2 Kings 23:22 records these words, "And the king commanded all the people, saying, Keep the Passover unto the LORD your God, as it is written in the book of this covenant." The key here is "as it is written in the book of the covenant." Josiah *immediately* and with *resolve* restored worship to its *biblical paradigm*. This is what Luther had done, and what Calvin had contended for in his polemic. This is true biblical reformation. This is where the reformers were simply practically applying Scripture to press into the kingdom of heaven.

Jesus was no less zealous for the institution of God's true worship in His house than these righteous kings were - He was *more* so. Jesus *began* His public ministry by cleansing the temple. In John 2:14-17 we have this account, "And He found in the temple those who sold oxen and sheep and doves, and the moneychangers doing business. When He had made a whip of cords, He drove them all out of the temple, with the sheep and the oxen, and poured out the changers' money and overturned the tables. And He said to those who sold doves, "Take these things away! Do not make My Father's house a house of merchandise!" Then His disciples remembered that it was written, "Zeal for Your house has eaten Me up." The modern evangelical church would never have succumbed to this. They would have set up a booth next to the other vendors, become their friends, and would have attempted to win them to the "truth" over a course of time by identification. Jesus, on the other hand, drove these men out with a whip. Why the contrast? Christ had an unmitigated zeal for the truth of the Word and a desire to see true worship instituted (*cf.* John 4:24). Immediately Christ overturned the "accepted" manner of worship and merchandising in the temple, to demonstrate the zeal, or fervor of spirit, for the worship of God. Reformation for Christ was immediate, and used a strategy to overthrow the *status quo* by building a new church through his apostles alongside of the corrupt church. In the cleansing of the temple, we see a departure from the false status of worship, to a recreation of the full reality of worship in the church that Christ came to build. Jesus had no time to waste, and in the course of three years taught his disciples to turn the world upside down, as Acts 17:6 says, "These that have turned the world upside down are come hither also."

For the modern church, and the modern Christian, there are many lessons to heed both from the Scriptures and the Reformers who implemented true biblical reformation. First, though more knowledge may flame more zeal and reform over time (as in the case with Luther) this does not mean the current evangelical knowledge obtained should lie dormant. Luther's Reformation was made up of a number of short bursts, or "little" reformations surrounding knowledge gained as he continued to study. As truths were made evident, they were implemented at all cost – even to his the peril of his own excommunication and death. To understand the truth surrounding any theological maxim, and to neglect imposing it in the life of the people, is sin (Rom. 14:23b; James 4:17). It should be agreed that prudence in implementation is necessary. But when the fundamentals of the faith are overthrown, and reformation surrounding those fundamentals are neglected though they be known by the Elders of the church, this is intolerable. If right worship, the right administration of the sacraments, and the exercise of biblical church discipline, are not set in the context of congregational life, it would be sin for the Elders to acquiesce to the congregation's theological ignorance. Implementation should be immediate.

Second, the Word of God is the only rule for faith and practice in the church where Jesus Christ is

Head. *The Westminster Confession of Faith* says, "But the acceptable way of worshiping the true God is instituted by himself, and so limited by his own revealed will, that he may not be worshiped according to the imaginations and devices of men, or the suggestions of Satan, under any visible representation, or any other way not prescribed in the Holy Scripture."[15] This parallels Calvin's argument throughout the *Necessity of Reforming the Church*. To add or take away from prescribed worship is sin. Ministers who compromise this principle to uphold a some regular aspect of their own fabricated worship compromise the integrity of the Word and their own convictions. Christians who compromise the truth are hypocrites.

Thirdly, in speaking to Christian ministers, those elders who fail to reform their church by implementing the Scriptures upon the life of the congregation compromise their own beliefs. Worship then becomes man-centered rather than Christ-centered. If they truly believed the Word of God, then right worship would necessarily be implemented by compulsion to obey God rather than please men.

---

[15] 1647 *Westminster Confession of Faith* 21:1.

Fourthly, speaking again to ministers, such elders cannot be church leaders by way of pretense. If Calvin had gone to Geneva to slowly reform the church, reform would have never taken place. His preaching, teaching, and catechistical instruction would have been hindered at every turn. He would not have been able to speak plainly and openly about the truth. Ministers must clearly and precisely make their theological convictions known to a church before they enter into it. The church should know precisely what changes will occur the moment the pastor enters the church. Anything less than this would be sin, and the pastor would be there in pretense. He would be a liar. He would lie to God, for not believing His Word enough to instigate it. He would lie to himself, for thinking that he believed a set of theological truths, when in fact, he really does not – for belief constitutes implementation and trust in those truths. He would be lying to the congregation by facade demonstrating a fabrication of false intentions in order to gradually win them over to the "truth" later on. It is forgotten by many that the father of lies is the devil. Such a position in terms of gradual reformation, is nothing but *devilish wiles*. If the Reformers had taken this position the Reformation would have never occurred. The Reformers would have died before they could have made any real implementations to the truth.

Fifthly, prudent reform takes place without the fear of men, and usually in the midst of contention. Burgess will point this out in detail later in the next section. But Luther and Calvin were consistently in the midst of conflict and difficulties due to the position they held to the truth. Recanting on revealed truth was not an option. Whenever sinful people are faced with the truth, disputation results. Such strife is impossible to avoid unless one compromises the truth. It may be after a long while that a congregation would mature in the truth, and such changes or implementations would be made more easily, but the historical record of the bible and the Reformation do not support this. Sinful people hate godly change. Calvin and Farel were expelled from Geneva for preaching their convictions and standing on the Word of God! Likewise, the moneychangers in the temple were not happy that Jesus overturned their tables. The religious leaders sought to kill Christ at every turn! Instead, theological compromise hopes that "later on" the church will understand the foundations of the faith so that the basics of worship, the sacraments, and discipline may be enacted successfully.

It would be wise imitating Hezekiah, Josiah, Luther, Calvin and the Lord Jesus Christ in the achievement of immediate reformation. Compromise is a *lie*. True Biblical Reformation for both the church and the Christian is biblically necessary. Gradual reformation in this regard is *intolerable*. It is intolerable both for the people of God who are deceived as to what real reformation and truth are about, and to the minister who compromises his beliefs, and neglects the honor of God's desire in true spiritual worship to become man-pleasers. May it be that true biblical reformation would be the norm, and sanctification would radically change the face of the church all over the world for the glory of Christ. Pray that true biblical reformation would affect the church, the home, the workplace, the state, the country your live in, in fact, all of society throughout the world for the glory of the great King, Jesus Christ, and the Kingdom of God.

finis

MEET ANTHONY BURGESS

By C. Matthew McMahon, Ph.D.

Taken in part from Smith's Selected Memoirs of the Scottish and English Divines, and Reid's Westminster Divines.

Anthony Burgess (1600-1663) was a very laborious and distinguished puritan divine. He was the son of a learned schoolmaster at Watford in Hartfordshire, and received his education in St. John's college, Cambridge.[16] From here he was chosen to a fellowship in Emanuel college, merely for his merit as a scholar. He was esteemed greatly in the university for his piety and learning, and likewise for his superior tutorship and powers of disputation. After his conversion and education Mr. Burgess became pastor of the church of Sutton Coldfield in Warwickshire; where his exemplary life, and conscientious labors, soon procured him an excellent reputation. He continued here diligently discharging the duties of his office, until the civil war had commenced, that the royal army, by plundering, insulting, and otherwise maltreating and

---

[16] In Watford Dr. Cornelius Burgess, and his successor Dr. John Burgess, was there, but Anthony was not a relative of either of them.

threatening him and his family, forced them to retire to Coventry for safety. The officers of the king's army were chiefly men of dissolute lives, who made a joke of religion; and the privates, having no regular pay, lived for the most part by plundering the people. When they took possession of a town, they rifled the houses of all who were accounted *puritans*; nor were they nice in their discriminations when occasions were pressing. Mr. Baxter says, "That after the battle of Edgehill, more than thirty worthy divines had retired to Coventry for safety from the soldiers and the fury of the rabble. The popular preachers, and persons of pious and godly lives, were the greatest sufferers; while such as prayed in their families, were heard singing psalms or repeating sermons, were accounted rebels, and most severely handled." At the time that Mr. Burgess fled to the garrison of Coventry, it was full of men of this description, who had a lecture every morning, in which service he took his regular course. About this time he was called to sit in the assembly of divines at *Westminster*, where he was generally and greatly esteemed for his solid learning and judicious deportment. He was repeatedly called to preach before the parliament at their fasts and other public occasions.

He was for some time preacher at Lawrencejury, and earnestly solicited, by the London ministers, to give a course of lectures against the antinomian errors of the times. These sermons were afterwards published at the request of the learned body at whose solicitation they had been given. "We, the president and fellows of Sion college, London, earnestly desire Mr. Anthony Burgess to publish in print his elaborate and judicious lectures upon the law and the covenants, against the antinomian errors of these times, which, at our entreaty, he hath preached, and for which we give him hearty thanks, so that the kingdom at large, as well as this city, may reap the benefits of those his learned labors. Dated at Sion college, June 11th 1646, at a general meeting of the ministers of London there assembled. Arthur Jackson, President, in name and by appointment of the rest."

In 1538, one John Agricola, a native of Eisleben, made a declaration of his sentiments, in which he maintained, that the law was neither fit to be proposed to the people as a rule of life, nor to be used in the church as a mean of instruction; and that the gospel alone ought to be inculcated and explained, both in the churches and in the schools. The followers of this man were called *antinomians*, from their opposition to the law. They hold, that the law has neither use nor obligation under the economy of grace; and the tenor of their doctrines evidently supersede the necessity of good works and a holy life. These antinomian tenets were greatly prevalent in England during and part of the seventeenth century. Dr. Crisp, who was born at London in 1600, was an enthusiastic asserter of these opinions; and the publication of his *Posthumous Works* occasioned a great amount of disputation in the country. But Mr. Burgess unmasked and refuted them in a most satisfactory manner by his lectures at Laurencejury.

Having finished his labors at London, he returned to discharge the duties of his pastoral office at Sutton Coldfield, where he remained until 1662. He was then ejected by the *act of conformity*; after which he spent the remainder of his days in great comfort, piety, and respect. Before he left his place, the new bishop of Coventry and Litchfield sent for him, as he also did for several other worthy divines of his diocese, hoping to gain them over to the prelatical order. Though he failed in his design, he was so candid as to express his good opinion concerning Mr. Burgess. He said, "That he was fit to fill a professor's chair in a university." Fuller says, in his account of Emanuel college, "Among the learned writers of this college I have omitted many who are still alive, as Mr. Anthony Burgess, the profitable expounder of the much mistaken nature of the two covenants." Dr. Wilkins enrolls him among the most eminent of the English divines for sermons and practical divinity. Dr. Cotton Mather says, in his Student and Preacher, "Of A. Burgess, I may say, he has wrote for thee excellent things." Mr. John Flavel, in his work *Fountain of Life*, sermon 2.5, says, that Mr. Anthony Burgess was a *grave* divine. Dr. John Wallis, who was a member of the Assembly of divines at Westminster, was his pupil, and gives him the following character: he says, "I was sent to the University of Cambridge, and there admitted in Emmanuel-College, under the tuition of Mr. Anthony Burgess, a pious, learned, and able scholar, a good disputant, a good tutor, an eminent preacher, a sound and orthodox divine, and afterward minister of Sutton-Coldfield, in Warwickshire."

His works are:

1. The Difficulties of, and Encouragements to, Reformation

2. Judgments Removed where Judgment is Executed
3. The Magistrate's Commission from Heaven
4. Rome's Cruelty and Apostasy
5. The Reformation of the Church more to be endeavored than that of the Commonwealth
6. Public Affections Pressed
7. Vindicaa Legis, or a Vindication of the Moral Law and the Covenants, from the errors of: Papists, Arminians, Socinians, and more especially Antinomians
8. The True Doctrine of Justification Asserted and Vindicated
9. A Treatise on Justification
10. Spiritual Refining
11. One hundred and forty-five Expository Sermons
12. The Doctrine of Original Sin
13. The Scripture Directory for Church Officers and People
14. Commentary on the whole first chapter of 2 Cor.

Meet Anthony Burgess

ORIGINAL TITLE PAGE

The Difficulty of,

and the Encouragements to

A REFORMATION.

A Sermon Preached before the Honorable House of
Commons

At the Public Fast, September 27, 1643

By

Anthony Burgess

Sometimes Fellow of Emmanuel College,
and now Pastor of Sutton-Cofield in Warwickshire

APPOINTMENT

It is this day ordered by the House of Commons assembled in Parliament, that Mr. Salloway due from this House gives thanks to Master Anthony Burgess for the great pains he took in the sermon he preached today (at the entreaty of this House) at St. Margarets in the City of Westminster, on this day of public humiliation. We desire him to print his sermon. And it is ordered that none prefers to print the aforementioned sermon but whom Mr. Burgess shall appoint under his handwriting.

H. Elsynge Clergy
Parliament D. Thomas Underhill

I appoint *Thomas Underhill* to print this sermon.
Anthony Burgess

Introductions

TO THE HONORABLE HOUSE OF COMMONS NOW ASSEMBLED IN PARLIAMENT

Worthy Patriots,

God has made you like the Brazen-Serpent; for those that have been flung with the serpents and dragons of Rome, have looked on you and been healed. You have overcome, and slain many difficult lions that have been in the way; yes, you have found *honey* in them.

The church is not in her travails and labor, as those strong women of Israel that could bring forth children alone. Therefore God has stirred you up to help her in her pangs. Therefore be courageous and do not languish in this great and necessary a work of *reformation*.

All truth is sweet, even natural truth; therefore the heathens in their sacrifice to Minerva (their Goddess of the Arts) offered honey, crying out, *truth is sweet*. But spiritual truths are sweeter than the honey and the honeycomb. This is the truth, even things that concern doctrine, discipline, and the worship of God, the godly desire to see practiced according to Scripture above all their works of reformation. You have this task in hand; you are to especially provide against the general ignorance in people by a solid and serious catechizing, and against the profaneness of people by powerful discipline, that so the sacraments may be dispensed comfortably. As in the kingdom, the lawyer, the physician and the tradesman can go comfortably in his calling. Therefore, provide that the *Pastor* also in the dispensation of ordinances may do it with joy, and not with grief. The heathens were careful about their idol sacrifices, *Prosul, O Prosul*, otherwise they would consider them profane. And we read in story, that the priest ready to sacrifice, asks this question, *who was there*? The answer was returned, *good and honest men*. And now in this work of reformation, go on exactly in the same way as good and honest men before God. Do not consult with flesh and blood. Do not leave in your building any nails or hooks standing out, that may tear those who go by. If you do so God may delight in your works. Labor to reform your own lives, and families, lest you be as the torch or candle that gives light to others, but consumes itself.

Your humble servant in Christ Jesus,
Anthony Burgess

Gradual Reformation Intolerable

A SERMON FOR THE HONORABLE HOUSE OF COMMONS AT THE PUBLIC FAST SEPTEMBER 27, 1643

THE TEXT OPENED

Mark 1:2-3, "As it is written in the Prophets, Behold I send my messenger before thy face, which shall prepare thy way before thee. The voice of one crying in the wilderness, Prepare ye the way of the Lord, make thy paths straight."

I will not begin my sermon, as commonly printers do their books, with some flowery or gaudy pictures on the first leaf, but fall immediately on that special matter which is contained in my text, and that cannot be handled rightly, unless I take in the former words, *The Beginning of the Gospel of Jesus Christ the Son of God*. In the whole context of these words, you have a proposition to be confirmed, and the argument confirming it. I call it proposition, and not a title or preface, such as that is, *the Revelation of John*, and in doing this I borrow gold of the Egyptian, (I mean) fetch my interpretation from a popish commentator, who had much learning and more malice. That my interpretation is more probable, consider the use of the word ευαγγέλιον. Some have taken it as signified in Scripture as *any joyful matter that is published*. Sometimes in particular, this is applied to the doctrine of Christ. Many have preached on this, seeing that in the Gospels it is the frequent use of the Word. But that idea of simply a "joyful matter", for the book and history of Christ, that is not a Bible sense, but an ecclesiastical. Even the evangelists in Scripture do not signify simply *one that makes the history of Christ*. We call the Gospels the four *evangelists* (though one *accompanied* the apostles in the preaching the Gospel). But we are not to take this simply as a matter of plain history, but that Gospel is here being *preached*. So when it follows, *the Gospel of Jesus Christ*, Jesus Christ is not the *matter* but the *author*. So the sense is the beginning of Christ's preaching was as it was foretold by the prophets. This being explained, you first have the manner of proving, which is by testimony, and although that is the weakest argument in human things, yet it is the strongest in divine. Secondly, there is the matter or proof itself. In clearing of all this, we might enter into two disputes; 1. In vindicating the author from perverting the meaning and scope of Isaiah, that the Jews would persuade us; 2. In answering the doubts about the diverse readings, whether it should be the prophets or in Isaiah only, which Beza contends for as the true reading. And this is made into such a great difficulty by Jerome, that he said he will crave pardon for his ignorance, as if the knot could not be untied. But should I handle these at large, you would say I gave a stone or serpent of *controversies* when you ask for the bread of nourishment. Therefore take this briefly as an explanation: the words in the text you shall find in Isaiah 40:3 (for those of Malachi tend to the same purpose) and are not to be understood only as the Jews would say. Here we have *the voice crying in the wilderness* to be the preaching of the Prophet that proclaimed the return of the Jews. But this is echoed typically of Christ and John the Baptist in their time, and consequentially to be applied to any time when Christ is coming graciously to deliver us from any such captivity.

So that from the manner of proving, and the matter or proof itself we will gather two *Doctrines* seasonable for *these* times.

THE DOCTRINE

Doctrine 1: That God's Word is the only rule and principle in matters of Religion and Reformation. It holds a *majority ad minus*, if the Prophets that were acted infallibly would yet confirm their matter delivered by Scripture, how much rather others would do this?

2. From the matter or argument, and in that, the *duty* pressed.

Doctrine 2: That it is a special duty on all, to remove all impediments, and to make way for Christ when he is coming to us.

We will begin with the first.

Doctrine: *The Word of God is the only rule and principle in matters of Religion or Reformation.*

It has the properties of a *rule*, which are these:

1. It is known and easy (Psa. 19:78). It is compared to a light, and a lantern to your feet. Nor will the evasion of the papists serve their turns, that it is light in itself, but not (as a light under the bushel; God should then do that, which our Savior says no man does) for that the Scripture is light effective as well as former appears by the addition, giving understanding to the simple. Besides, to be a light in itself is a kind of contradiction, seeing the light it has *is* for us. It is true indeed, there is a two-fold obscurity, one of matter, which sometimes is so excellent and perfect, that our understanding cannot reach, and so in this sense it is said, *the natural man perceives not the things of God*. There is a natural man, one that does *excolore animam*, such as Aristotle and Tully, But this blame is to be cast on our understanding, not the Scripture. We say, the sun is most visible, and God most easy to be known, because the one has the greatest motive of seeing which is light; and the other of being understood, which is verity; so are these truths most full of light, if our understandings are opened. The second obscurity is of the phrase, and that the Scripture does not use in things essential to salvation.

Commonly what is obscurely set down in one place is clear in another. Shall not the Spirit of God which gives a clear understanding and expressions to men actually be clear? See the papists folly. They hold it possible to fulfill the Law, but not to understand it. When we urge that place, Deut. 30:12, the Word *is not hidden from You, and it is very close to you.* O! they say, this is to be understood of the fulfilling of the Law, not knowing it. But this is buffoonery. We conclude then, according to Scripture, the Holy Scriptures *are* the holy ladders, by which we climb up into heaven, and know God's meaning.

2. It is infallible and certain. The infallibility of it is witnessed by those places where God's Word is compared to *gold seven times refined*, and where it is said, "Heaven and earth shall sooner pass away, but my words shall not pass away," (Matt. 24:35). Not one jot or tittle shall pass away. And so, the Scriptures say, "thy testimonies are sure." By all this it appears, that the Word of God is a *fixed Canon*. It cannot be wrested and wyer-drawn, so as to approve one thing today, and the contrary tomorrow. It is hellish blasphemy to compare it to a nose of wax; and to say that it is to be

interpreted, as the condition of the Church alters, so must the Scripture alter. By this delusion they confirm with what Tertullian said, *God shall not be God unless man please*. If you say that the Apostle Peter speaks of some who wrested the Scripture, and put it on the torture rack, this is to be granted concerning the words, not the sense and matter of the Holy Spirit intended by those words. That is invariable and cannot be a reed shaken with every wind of interpretation. Simply because heretics would fly to the words and deny the sense, they say the Church of God is confirmed to use *new words* to distinguish them by. But this is nonsense. Irenaeus compares heretics to the hyena that imitates the Shepherds voice, and so by that means seduces the sheep into destruction. Let us stand on the infallibility of the Word of God and not men's delusions. This infallibility of the Word is so great, that when some, as Saul and Uzziah, have gone against it, as if their special considerations might give them protection, (which may have been indeed fair and plausible), yet they were severely punished by God.

3. It is universal in regard of time, place, and persons, so that he is the true and good Catholic that keeps to this

Catholic rule.[17] The word was never a rule to declare to the Church anything besides that we have received. Therefore in the Old Testament, Isaiah 8:20 says, "To the Law and to the testimony; if they speak not according to this, it is because there is no light in them." Therefore also good kings Hezekiah and Josiah were guided by this pillar of fire when they set on the work of *Reformation*. It was also a rule in the New Testament, therefore our Savior often comments on it (Luke 10:26, Psa. 40:7), "What is your reading of it? And in the scroll of the book it is written of me?" When Paul would reform the abuses crept in the Church of Corinth about the *Sacrament*, he goes to the first institution and as it was delivered from Christ. And if we consult with the Fathers, we shall find that this Scripture was the running brook out of which they gathered those stones which they flung in the forehead of those *Goliaths* that oppressed the truth. There was never any error, but it went up and down, like Cain, from one place to another, fearing lest every place is as the sun in the firmament is light for the whole world (not only for this Kingdom, or that, but for nations). So God's Word is a rule to England, to Scotland, to Rome,

---

[17] *Catholic* in this sense means universal Christian.

to all where it is promulgated. Lastly, it is universal to all persons, for as the Psalmist said of the Sun, "there is nothing hid from the heat thereof;" so *no* person or persons are exempted from the obligation of the Word. There is none too great to have his faith and life controlled by it. Therefore it is able to make the man of God wise to salvation, *cf.* 1 Timothy 3:17. But not only a minister, but the whole council; yes, this is the rule that binds *Kings and Parliaments*. We must all stoop to the Word.

4. It is indivisible. When we say a rule is *indivisible* the meaning is that nothing may be added to it, or detracted from it, and this is specifically what the Scripture states in closing of all, "For I testify unto every man that heareth the words of the prophecy of this book, If any man shall add unto these things, God shall add unto him the plagues that are written in this book: And if any man shall take away from the words of the book of this prophecy, God shall take away his part out of the book of life, and out of the holy city, and from the things which are written in this book," (Rev. 22:18-19). It is a challenge to itself; how great a breach of this truth was been made when the *Apocryphal* books, and

many other *traditions* and *ceremonies* have been equalized to Scripture, and made as necessary as the Bible? No, is there not such folly in people that they are as willing to be without God's Word as man's inventions? It is a necessary truth, which all magistrates, all ministers, all people should believe, *that God's Word is perfect.* We must understand that there is *enough* in it as a rule to direct and work holiness in us. How wretched then are the papists that will have images, and this like the *Layman's Bible*, as if God's word were *not* enough. Take heed of their perverse disputings. They will not have the Scripture read in the known tongue, lest people through mistake, make errors. Yet, they have images which are suffered by them, and through them they naturally teach *idolatry*. When therefore these traditions and ceremonies climb up like Reuben into his father's bed, let them lose all their glory. The Word of God is Hebrews 9:15, *alibi*, called a *testament*. Now you know that to a man's will nothing maybe added, nor anything detracted. And this you will always find to be true: all subversion of true faith and pure worship flows from this – it is either because something of Scripture is *neglected* or something that is not Scripture is *introduced*.

5. It is adequately proportionable to our faith. The rule and the thing regulated must be fitted one to another, faith and the Word of God must run parallel. All that is written must be believed must be written. O! that the church of God had in all ages kept to the Scripture as Ruth to Naomi, where the one lives the other would, and where the one dies the other will. *I do not believe it because I do not read it*, was a known proverb in antiquity. *Thou art to say, here you shall go O my Faith, and no further; Here you shall go O my worship, and no further*, this we first believe when we do believe, that we ought to believe nothing beyond Scripture. This also is to be extended to your practice and conversation. As you are to take no religion then what the Scripture allows, so you are neither to live any other life then what the word commands. Therefore come you who live a profane and wretched life. Let us expostulate with you. You are no papist, so will you *not* hold to transubstantiation, why? Is not God's word against profaneness as well as popery? If this were attended to, men would have holy lives as well as sound judgments.

6. And lastly, a rule must be first, and before the thing to be regulated. A rule is a measure, and therefore must

be first in its kind. To question whether the church should be before the Scripture is to question whether *man* is before God. This is true, divines well observe, that the Scripture may be considered either in respect of the outward form, as it is a writing, or in respect of the inward form and its sense, as it is the Word of God. Now in the letter sense, God's Word was always before a Church, because by the word we are begotten again, and so *made* the church. Therefore it is that God's word is more ancient then churches and fathers, and this is the antiquity we should set up. It is true, the church in regard of her ministry, and leading us to believe, is before the Scripture, but we never put forth a divine holy faith until the Spirit of God works our assent to his word because it is *his word*. So to stay in the authority of *the church* instead of the word, is to stay in John the Baptist, that bore witness of Christ, and not go to Christ himself. Some might say, seeing therefore the Word of God is most ancient, why should men press us in faith or worship, to go and see what was done 500 or 600 or 2000 years ago, and not rather go to the Scripture which was before this? But as the owl and the thief cannot endure the light, so neither can error or superstition the Word of God.

CAUTIONS

Now take these *cautions*,

1. First, the Word of God is the *only* rule. In popery they share with God in everything; to grace they join free will, to Christ's merits their own merits to God, angels and saints, to the Scriptures their traditions, and Church authority. This is urged so precisely that if the Church determines an error to be a truth, yet they are bound to believe it. They even *merit* by believing it. This is how it was among the Sadducees and Rabbis, if their elders said the right hand were the left, or the left the right, they *must* assent to it. If we would be content with this, that the Scripture were *a half rule* all would be well, but as God is a *perfect* God, so is His Word it is a perfect Word. We must have no other gods besides Him, so also no other Scripture or word beside this. Do not then in matters of religion make this (what others say) your compass to fail by, or make it your custom based on men's imaginations. Go to the word and ask, "What does God's Word say in all this?" Are not political considerations a rule to many people? Is not custom a rule to many? "Woe to thee, O thou torrent of custom, who is able to resist thee?" cries Augustine. It

is true if this is received, here will appear a much nicer and singular aim toward the loud cries for a *reformation*. This reformation the world hates. The world is not able to bear this exhortation, "Let the Word of God rule you, let the Word of God reform you."

2. When we say it is *a rule*, it must be extended to that end for which it is a rule. As the Scripture is not a rule to physicians or mathematicians in their proper arts, so neither does it particularly tend to this or that individual action for all essentials. It is a rule, a general rule, for circumstances. Nor does this detract from the perfection of the Scripture, that it does not command every circumstance. A thing is imperfect when it lacks some perfection that is due to it. It is not an imperfection in the body that is not everywhere, because this is not requisite to the body. So neither is it to be expected from the Scripture, that *all* circumstances must be by *name* commanded. It is true, the church must take heed that under the name of circumstances she does not bring in *worship*, which has been always the subtitles of Satan. In this way altar worship and image worship were made *circumstances* in men's books by distinctions, but in their practice as

much as God's own instituted worship. Be sure to give enough to the Scriptures. *I adore the Scriptures fullness,* Bonaventure said meaning that if he were to make an error, he would rather error in giving too much to grace, then to free will. So you should do the same thing in giving too much to the Scripture, rather than too little, though it is best to go neither to the right hand nor the left.

3. Though it is a rule, yet it does not exclude other ministerial helps. Here we consider the office of pastors and teachers, as also of praying to God, and the diligent reading of God's Word. Therefore it is a vain and absurd question of the papists when they say, "Let a man be locked up in a study with a Bible, what good will he get by that if he cannot read!" As if they are saying because we say it is a rule, therefore other ministerial helps are not necessary. The pastors and teachers indeed have a light, yet as God when He created the world, he conveyed the whole light of the world into the body of the sun, so that though the moon and stars should give light, yet they should shine with no other light but what they received from the sun. So God in the constitution of the church, conveyed

its whole light into the Scripture, and the offices of the Church are to shine with light *from there*. The godly pastors and teachers of the Church do not *make truths*, though they may *declare them*; as Solomon did by his prudence did not *make* the child the true mother's child but *declared* it; and the skillful jeweler does not *make* the jewel, but does distinguish it from counterfeit jewels.

FAITH

This rule extends first, to matters of faith.

A sound faith is the soul of religion, it is like the sun in the firmament, like the eye in the body; and commonly, an ill faith and ill life goes together. Therefore Hymenaeus and Philetus, as they made shipwreck of the faith, so they did also of *a good conscience*, 1 Timothy 2:17. There is no building of any confessions of faith unless the materials are fetched from this mountain. Error and heresy have no such enemy as the Scripture. The holy Fathers were scrupulous in using the word *homoasios* and Trinity, and all because they were not Scriptural words quoted in the text. Therefore heretics are owls that cannot endure the light. Lindan the Papist was not ashamed to say, "That it had been better for the Church if there had been no Scripture at all, but only traditions." Now we have seen that Scripture is the solid ground on which we believe. So even though we may be as orthodox in doctrine as can be, yet if it is not *because* of Scripture, it is but a human faith that we create. As men may have a human repentance (when their hearts are troubled) merely on human considerations, which is *far* from godly sorrow, so we may have a human faith, merely because of education and human custom; and all this comes *far* short of divine faith.

WORSHIP AND DISCIPLINE

Secondly, let us consider *worship* and *discipline*. An Orthodox Church without good discipline and pure worship is like a field of corn without hedges. What a comely Church should we have if the orders and commands of Scripture were looked too? In worship, all that is done without God's Word, is doing we do not know, John 4:22 "You worship you know not what." And by what ground they receive one voluntary act of worship, they might receive *more*. The pope once resolved that he with his cardinals should at a set time ride on asses partly to show their humility, and partly to imitate Christ's riding on an ass to Jerusalem. But the cardinals refused it as being too absurd. Yet they might *on the same ground* have received that as a custom, as *all* their other rabble of worship. So for discipline and order of worship, a profane man should be as rare in the church as a blazing flare, "If any one be an idolater, a reviler, do not to eat with such an one," (1 Corinthians 6:11). And again, "If any walk disorderly, withdraw from such an one." I know different judgments improve these places to different opinions, but I press that which all agree in. I acknowledge that governors are more to be encouraged in this work, because the ignorance and profaneness of people cannot endure to see a brazen serpent broken down. You worthy patriots, you have endeavored to bury Moses' body, lest it should be worshipped and how does the devil withstand you?

LIVING HOLY

Thirdly, to our outward conversation, Psalm 19, "By them thy servant is forewarned". The Scripture is the antidote against sin, *cf.* Psalm 119:9. A young man may cleanse his ways by them, in the former a king, in the latter a young man. Where there are the greatest temptations, even there God's Word will prevent. Now this use of the Scripture men do not consider. They do not dare have any other faith then the Scripture propounds; and yet they do not dare live another life. Therefore you believe *as it is written*, so, live and fear and be filled with joy *as it is written*. Can you prove your drunkenness lawful, more than your heresy?

Fourthly, consider the heart and conscience of man. In this there is a difference from all other rules and laws. Those bind only the outward man, but these reach to the heart and conscience, *cf.* Romans 7. The law is spiritual, it even convinces a self-admiring Pharisee. When this sunlight shines, it discovers all the hidden thoughts of the heart (all those moats) that otherwise would not be seen. So Hebrews 4:12 says, "It's a two-edged sword..." The eloquence and wit of men do not awe and terrify the conscience, but the Word of God does. Scripture makes the heart cry out, *I am overcome,*

overcome. Its true God makes use of human eloquence, but all must be subordinate to the Word. As God is the Father of spirits, so the Word is a word of spirits. If the word comforts, though the world threatens, the heart bears up itself. But if the word of God threatens, the heart is discouraged due to it.

USE 1. OF EXHORTATION TO SET UP THIS RULE.

"Let the Word of God dwell in you", follow that in your reformations, as the wise men did the star. You are careful (as magistrates) to keep parliamentary privileges, but be as tender about Scripture privileges for this is your spiritual *Magna Carta*. Then will God set you up in the consciences of men, when they shall see that you are as seriously bent to keep God's right as your own. Isaiah 8:19, "Should not a people inquire of their God?" Every nation seeks to their own god; the gluttonous man takes counsel from his belly, the ambitious from his great ones, the papist from the pope's chair, and shall not we from *God*? It was the complaint of an anonymous person in his epistle to Calvin, (we hope through the blessing of God this

Parliament will take it away) concerning the disorders in our discipline and church, says, "We go to the nobles and great men to redress this abuse, they answer, they cannot do anything unless there were a public constitution of the realm for it. But when that public Senate is called, there are so many civil businesses to be handled, that the cause of Christ is always neglected." Therefore we, as the ministers of God's Word, are like John the Baptist, a voice crying out to you, *Prepare ye the way for the Lord*; and that by his Word. It was said of the people of Israel, that there was an ounce of that calf they made in every punishment that fell on them. And may not we say that the general neglect of discipline has had a great share in all our sins and punishments? O you blessed fathers, who were afraid to use the word trinity, and the like, because it was not in Scripture, how could you lie still in your graves for these years past, and not rather haunt us as ghosts, who had so much of doctrine and of worship that had no Scripture for them?

Now there are other rules set up by men.

1. Antiquity: This is the Gorgon's head that all superstitious men hold up, thinking to silence all men immediately, whereas indeed they deal as the Gibeonites did, who came with their moldy bread and old shoes which they had newly received, as if they had enjoyed them a long while. So it is with most of their old traditions, and their moldy inventions, which they obtrude on us. But how many things are improved? Are not your states, your revenues improved? and shall not the light and gifts that God has given be improved? Is it not Augustine's observation, that the epistle of the fathers were mended by provincial counsels, and provincial by universal, and the first universal by the latter. Make a note of that, the first by the latter; so that what is said of natural old age, may sometimes be true of ecclesiastic, *ipsa senectus morbus (old age is a disease)*. It was the observation of an acute wit, that time was like the river of waters that bore up all the frothy and empty things, but all the ponderous things sunk and were seen no more.

2. Custom: This is a rule seen more often than not, and by far too many in the church; *this we and our fathers have been used to do.* Now how vain is this? For by the same

season heathens and pagans might plead for their idolatry. Yes, Symmachus did when he entreated the emperor not to bring in Christian religion; O!, he says, *sequendi sunt parentes, qui sequante sunt feliciter suos, cont meliosa est emendatio sene utis: our fathers lived quietly doing this and thus, it is a reproachful thing to be wiser than our fathers.* And this is the great mountain in the way of reformation – customs. Though these customs might be so ridiculous, though never so dangerous, yet they will stand for them. Augustine tells us that he came into a city where the people had a custom on one day in a year to meet together, and to throw stones at one another, by which many were killed, yet because it was a custom, he could not make them leave it.

3. Fathers: in this way the papists were the fathers of this new religion. Now although it is true, that our learned divines prove all our orthodox positions out of the early fathers, yet they in turn rely on our Savior, and rest upon his authority. And indeed there are hardly any throughout the history of the church which set forth the fullness of the Scripture more than they do. It was the insolent speech of that proud heretic Dioscorus, *I am cast out with the fathers*; so let any error, any

will worship be cast out of the church. Then the cry is, *this is cast out with the fathers.* Keep in mind, the father's works are uncertain, and many times they contradict one another, yes even themselves sometimes. But how can they be rules as the papists maintain?

4. The name of a church: this is another rule to many. People are of the faith which the church they live in professes. This has been the Goliath's sword for people. It was Erasmus' speech, as Gerhard cites him, that the church had so much authority over him, and he gave so much to it, that if she should conclude that the Arian and Pelagian opinions are the true faith, he would believe it. What? Do you go against the church? Where if you asked, what is the church? It would have been found to have been nothing but the will and resolution of a proud pope, for he is the papist's virtual church. It is true, the authority of a church that is holy and true ought to work much spiritual good on men. "We," the apostle says, "nor the church of God have no such custom;" and therefore that is commendable, *Contra rationem nemo sobrius, contra scripturam nemo Christiannus, contra ecclesiam nemo pacificus.* But then he still provided that the church shines with the light of Scripture. The

authority of the right church must not be a cipher, and yet must not be all things. To keep church government from tyranny, and Christian liberty from a Socinian doubting, is very hard.

5. Reason. And this has been extolled much by a Socinian party, but they confound the instrument and the rule together; reason is the instrument applying, not the rule itself, and they are not reason's truths, but Scripture truths. As the artificer beats out his golden metal into such and such forms, it is not the hammer's gold, but only the hammer forms it. And as they argue against Scripture, that one interprets it in one way, and another in another way, so we may say of reason, this is right reason to one, that is not to another. *Tu hereticus mihi, & ego tibi.* Especially make note of this, that all reason severed from God's Word is corrupt and carnal, a very ill judge in the worship of God and our conversation and spiritual walk.

6. Universality: To do as the most do. This is a great rule among the lost. They never consider what the Scriptures direct to, but they will believe, and worship, and live as most do. Now God has expressly forbidden

this, "Thou shall not follow a multitude to do evil." There are but few to whom Christ reveals himself. "The whole world lies in darkness." And as the earth's mold turns into stones is far greater than that which becomes metal, and as the weeds are far more than the flowers, so are sinners far more than those that do truly worship God. This sect of "Christ's way" is everywhere spoken against. Christ says, "And you shall be hated of all men for my name's sake." But as hell is not more comfortable because so many are there, so neither ought the paths there to be the more pleasant because there are so many companions which lead to destruction.

7. Enthusiasm: That is, when men set up their private fancies and spirits against the meaning of God in his Word. But because all the godly are traduced by following a private spirit, and because that place of Scripture is urged by some, "...no Scripture is of private interpretation," it is good to consider the distinction I shall bring grant that it be read as signifying an *impulse*, or something coming on us. An interpretation may be said to be private either, 1. in regard of the person, and so that is not forbidden; for it is lawful for one private

man to gainsay the whole world, if he has a true interpretation of Scripture; or 2. it is private *ratione medii*, when he takes a false medium. He does not take the context, and the circumstances, *etc*. And this private interpretation, which does not publicly appear in the words, is forbidden. Or 3. private is *ratione finis*, the end of a man, when though he takes a right way and course, yet he has some sinister end, and this also is forbidden. So then, a private spirit is then made *a rule* when we take our own thoughts of the Scripture and do not found or establish our meaning on the context. The papists and enthusiasts are contrary in this to one another. This Christ, as Tertullian says, is always crucified between two thieves, truth suffers between two contrary errors.

CONSEQUENCES

Now if we follow scripture rules, consequences flow from it.

1. Such a man will be sure and constant in his way; for as the truth is yesterday and today, the same *forever*, so also will the frame and temper of the man be the same

forever. A man that does not build on Scripture has a weekly and a monthly faith that comes and goes, ebbs and flows when he has need, or not. Therefore, we see the importance of those phrases, "Hold fast the words of Life," (Titus 1:8). *The godly men* (Fox says) *were called the just, and the hold-fast men, because they would not abate of the least tittle they held.* It was a proverb to express the difficulty of a thing by saying that you cannot reach a man with Jesus Christ. Where men that have not built on this foundation, they are like Theophilus, Bishop of Alexandria, who was nicknamed Euripus, because of his ebbing and flowing in matters of religion; for a bishopric he would swear to the Nicene Counsel, and then to keep it he would forswear it again.

2. He will be holy and spiritual in his conversation; for such as those rules are, such will he be. The Scriptures are called *holy*, not only because the matter of them is holy, and the efficient author of them holy, but because the end and effect of them is to make us holy. They will not only make a man orthodox in judgment, but right in affections and conversations also. Therefore, it is that there is as little holiness in the lives of the papists as there is found faith in their judgments. How can it be

otherwise, seeing the church of Rome has dealt with the people of God, as if a man would commit a ship into the sea without pilot, compass, or sails, and so venture it into the ocean? And this Scripture's holiness does as far surpass that which people call *piety*, as the sun does the glowworm.

3. This will bring peace and security to him, and to the kingdom that receives it. As many as walk according to this rule, *peace be unto them*, Galatians 6:16. Ignorant and profane people cry out. It is this crying for Scripture so much that makes all this trouble. But look at the contrary, in 2 Chronicles 5:35, "When there was no teaching priests, nor the law in Israel, then there was trouble to him that went in and went out." Again, 2 Chronicles 17:9-10, this is when Jehoshaphat reformed according to God, then all was quiet, and fear fell on all the nations round about. The bringing in of God's word, and a Scripture reformation, is like the bringing in of the Ark of God to Obededom's house; it carries much blessing with it.

4. This Scripture man will be accounted nice and scrupulous. If you regard this conscience, which

attends only God's word, it must necessarily be nice and scrupulous in the world's account, that as they wonder you do not run into the same excess of riot with them, so also that you cannot use all such worship and receive all such traditions as they do. A tender constitution feels the least blast of wind, so also does a tender heart. Look on the carriage of our Savior's not washing his hands, it was but a civil thing, he knew how much the neglect of this would prejudice him, and yet he would not do it. For as he will have a liberty of conscience where some are superstitiously fearful, so again he will have a holy fear of conscience, where others are desperately bold. Never then let reformers startle at this, to be thought more strict then necessary.

5. He will be judged in a singular manner from others. This arises from the other, for seeing his conscience is so tender, then also his life will be disagreeing to the most, as the apostle's rule, Romans 12:2, not to fashion ourselves according to this world. Here we remember James 1:28 where the apostle says that *pure religion* is to keep ourselves unspotted from the world. It is true on the other side, if there is an irregularity, it is in most men of the world that they do not conform to the Word

of God which is the rule, for the godly do as they should do; as in a pasture where there is a flock of sheep, if all but two or three break the hedges and run into the highways, who are wanderers? The multitude? No, those two or three that abide in the pastures.

6. It will make him become hated and abhorred of all, "You shall be hated of all men for my name's sake." Therefore the papists, because we reformers would have all our doctrine decided *by Scripture*, call us *Scriptuarios*, and *atramentarios Theologos*, Inky Divines. To be a *bible-bearing puritan* was matter of scoff. How would the fire of Chrysostom have kindled against these wretches, who on that place in Scripture, "Let the Word of God dwell plentifully in you," (Colossians 3:16), cries out, *Hearken all you tradesmen, get bibles.* This undoes you, that you think it belongs only to some special men to read the Scripture. And how can it be but that the world must hate this, seeing there is such a contrariety between a life of Scripture, and the life of carnal men? A Scriptural conversation, and a Scriptural reformation can be no more endured by the world then David by Saul because the pulling down of one is the

establishing of the other. *Semper aliena virtus formidolosa est*, one man's virtue makes him that lacks it afraid.

But how may we get to be a better Christian by this rule?

1. We must be frequent in it. See Colossians 3, "Let it dwell in you," for you must know it, and be as familiar with it as your own houses. You must do it plentifully, that is, both for the object and subject. The object is to know it all, not just this or that parcel of the Word of God; the *whole* Scripture. And then for the subject, in all the parts of the soul, the understanding, the will and the affections it must be like Aaron's oil running down from the head to the feet. Therefore, God would have the king himself to write his word with his own hand, that so he may be acquainted with it, and rule accordingly, (see Deuteronomy 17).

2. Pray for understanding. Only a spiritual understanding and a heavenly eye can discern an excellency in the Scripture. It argued a profane spirit in Polutian, who said there was more in one of Pindar's odes, then all David's Psalms. But David prayed that

God would open his eyes, that he might see the wonderful things in *God's law*. All truth is sweet, but the truth of Scripture is sweet above everything else. Men may read the Scripture, write commentary on it, and yet not have a spiritual and savory understanding of it. *Nunquam Pauli mentem intelliges, nisi prins Pauli spiritum imbibiris, unless God give thee the heavenly spirit of Paul, you will never understand the heavenly meaning of Paul.*

3. Be humble and meek, submitting to the simplicity contained in it. To the humble God will teach his ways. It is a great matter to stoop to the Scripture. Augustine complains of this, that *luerarum sypho tumidus*, swelling with pride of human learning, he refused the simplicity of the Scriptures. Bradwardine, speaking of himself before he felt the power of grace on his heart, said that he was much offended when he heard Paul read in the church. Why? He said because he had no *metaphysicum ingenium (metaphysical character)*. In this proud men seldom ever come to know the truth. God hides these things from the prudent and wise of the world.

4. Get a great love for God's truth. And this is the reason of all antichristian errors, and believing such lies

as they do. Why? Because they do not receive God's word and do not love it. They loathed this manna, and therefore God makes a famine among them. There is no more terrible *prognostique* of God's delivering up a people to blindness and hardness, then they are rejecting of his Word. We are to take heed how we reject God's reformation, lest he swear in his wrath, that we shall never be reformed. What is the great sin which cries out today for England? Even a hatred of God's truth. They do not love its power and purity, but as the Gadarenes had rather have their swine then Christ's presence, so these want to have their brutish lusts rather than God's truth. God removes these means of grace when people are incurable, as when the patient is dead, all the physical boxes and cups are taken away.

THREE THINGS WHICH ARE NECESSARY

Now that the Word of God may be set up, these three things are necessary:

1. To encourage *preaching*; which is that great work so severely charged on the ministers. Hezekiah spoke

comfortably to those that taught the good knowledge of God. There was a very noxious and destructive opinion, that *reading* was *preaching*. The question is not whether reading may not in some sense be *called* preaching, (taking preaching for any declaration of God's truth). But we are making the distinction that reading is not *ministerial preaching*. When the apostle Paul says he must *divide God's word aright*, does he simple mean that ministers are to read the Word of God, or is there more to it than that? When Paul says, "who is sufficient for these things," does he mean, who is able to read? When he says, "Give thyself to study, that thy profiting may appear to all men," does he mean that all men should see that you read the Scriptures to people better than they did? No, reading and commenting on Scripture is not *preaching* the Word. It is more than a comment. It is more than reading.

2. Catechizing. This would do good both to minister and people. First, it does good to the minister. There is a memorable story that which Chemnitins relates of his master Chytreus. When he read over diverse authors, and devoured many volumes, he set himself to prove the catechistical points of divinity by Scripture, and

then he found himself in a new world and was not able to do it; in other words, as for the minister, so much more for the people. Who will give us to weep rivers of tears for the general ignorance in all parishes and congregations? Bellarmine says that faith may be defined better by ignorance then knowledge. This is true, that the faith of the common people (such as it is) may be so defined. Help the church of God, O you worthies, in this.

3. Encouraging learning, and the knowledge of the language of Scripture. Whatever translations may be good, yet in regard of the emphasis of the original, we may say as the Queen of Sheba to Solomon, *that which she heard was nothing to the glory she saw*. Then came in the stated error and superstition that it was heresy, or at least suspicious of it, to understand Greek and Hebrew. A divine ought to be that which was said of Nazianzene, *an ocean of divinity*.

THE TESTIMONY ITSELF

We come now to the testimony itself, "Prepare ye the way of the Lord," *etc.*, which contains the effect of

John's ministry, as also the duty of his hearers who were fallen into a corrupt time, when the Philistines had filled up all the wells the Pharisees and scribes had corrupted the Word of God by false interpretations. The Greek word for *he will prepare*, and ετοιμάζω, *prepare yea*, are taken from the custom of great ones, who used to have a way made for them. Or as others, when great commanders were to lead an army, they sent someone before, who were called *edetieroi* that made level the way. The Hebrew counterpart word is emphatic, which signifies such a *removal of all offensive things*, that the *face may no longer behold them.*

And therefore we observe that:

It is the duty of a people to remove all difficulties and oppositions in the way, that so Christ may come and dwell with them. The text takes it either literally to take everything away that may stop their speedy return from Babylon, or typically, what should oppose the spiritual restoration of the church, by the Messiah. This is to be done proportionally, for whatsoever mountain or valley may be in the way, where Christ is coming, it is to be removed. When Christ had his triumphal entry, they threw garments in the way, and with much acclamation cried, "Hosanna, Blessed he be that cometh in the name of the Lord;" so are we with all earnest affection to cry, "Blessed be that reformation, which cometh in the name of the Lord." The Psalmist also cries out about this, "Lift up your heads ye gates, that the king of glory may come in," (Psalm 24:7).

HINDRANCES TO REFORM

We will first show what are the impediments, the hills and valleys, that hinder Christ's coming to reign in his church.

1. A corrupt judgment, as if there were no necessity of preparation of reformation. That was Laodicea's case. She was full of herself, and rich, therefore she is counseled to buy *eye salve*, Revelation 3:18. In this way the Church of Rome is in a desperate disease, because she thinks she cannot be sick, and that she cannot err. In this way all reformation is accounted needless. What else should we necessarily do? So many churches would have been more pure and reformed if they had not thought themselves *reformed enough* and therefore as for

a particular person, Paul says, "I had not known sin, had not the law said, Thou shalt not lust." So also may a church should say, *I had not known this to be an abuse, this to be error, had not the Scripture manifested it.*

2. Attending to carnal policy. This makes men vary according to state consideration. There are many men that can place their consciences, as Diogenes bragged he could do to his tub, wherever the wind blew the waves, he said he could turn the mouth of his barrel from it. There are a certain people spoken of in a story, that worship no set god, but the first thing they met with, *Hodie tu Jupiter este, cras mihi truneus eris,* Today this shall be good divinity, tomorrow error, today this shall be a reformation, tomorrow turbulence. This carnal respect is a loadstone to many, *Fac me Episcopum Romanum, Christianus,* make me bishop of Rome and I'll be a Christian. There are some who thought gain was godliness; how many children of Balaam are there who may be hired to curse the people of God?

3. A sinful symbolizing moderation. How hard a matter is it, not to take a lame and half reformation? *Si dimidio Christo essemus contenti, facile transigremus omnis,* all quarrels

would soon end if we would take up with a half Christ, Calvin said. *Let the child be divided*, the false mother says to Solomon. *Purge out the old leaven*, Chrysostom ponders that when he says "thoroughly and fully." And Peter Martyr follows this of Chrysostom. *In reformation there are our principles ad mult connivendum est, li ist agendum; sed alia est severitas verbi Divini, We must wink at many things, and proceed gently, but the severity of God's word is another matter of thing.* But you will say, *Shall there be no moderation, must we all be like frogs that cannot go, but leap?* Yes, there is a lawful moderation, but here we condemn a sinful symbolizing one.

4. Love to earthly things. If you read the prophet Haggai, you will find that the care and love to build their own houses at that time than in the spiritual beauty of ordinances. When people have more joy in their hearts, by the increasing of wine and oil, than in God and his ways, it is no wonder if so few make way for Christ. It was Nazianzens' excellent temper to thank God he had anything to lose for Christ's sake.

5. A fifth impediment to reformation is profaneness and license in wickedness. This is that which troubles men

so much. Men should not be so merry in their lusts and their sins. But this thought should comfort the Christian. Christ endured the contradiction of sinners. This comforted Christians before in times past as Tertullian notes, "Who are they that speak against us, but the ale houses and brothel houses?" You may ask, "What is the good we would do, that the mouths of the bad are so open?" Therefore, it is that men are patient under all popish burdens, because these and their lusts may stand together. But when Christ comes, then they will rage, crying, *Let us break his bonds.* It is a torment to wicked spirits that they cannot be wicked, as they have been, Matthew 8:29, "Why art thou come to torment us before our time;" what torment could that be to the devil, to be cast out of the possessed bodies? Yes great, because they could not vex and destroy as before. So a reformation comes and torments proud church governors, and why so? Because they cannot oppress and rage as they use to do.

6. The general opposing and disliking of it by people. This is a great stop in the way of reformation. Why should just a few stir for and against the current of men's desire, especially if many great, and many learned

rise up against it? This difficulty Martin Luther confessed was no little temptation to him. *Tune solus sapis? totne errant universi? Are thou only wise, are all others in an error?* But if this were to be regarded, then neither prophets, nor Christ, nor Luther, nor Calvin, should have set on any reformation. For the world could not bear them. Always reformations have been judged impossible things; *Abi in cellam, & dic, miserere nostri,* as one said to Luther, *go and pray in thy cell, for thou art not likely to do anything by stirring.* So Psalm 2 says, "Why do the people rage and take counsel together," that Christ may not be exalted on his throne. But this will not be a good excuse. It is better to endure the rage of people then the anger of God; better to have the world frown on you, then God frown on you.

7. The seeming newness that is in it. Indeed, truth is before error; it is for our sins that truth is new. It argues our deep apostasy and revolting sin that the orders and ways of Christ should be new. Profane people should not lift up their heads so high among Christians. It was not so from the beginning. It is a novel thing to be erroneous or superstitious. Here people break the Sabbath, neglect piety, *etc.* These things to them are

new things. It is strange to consider how doting men are of the old ways they have lived in, though never taken up a first on any Scriptural consideration. See the corruptions of men's hearts. See that they are not interested in a new reformation for godliness, but new fashions are admired, superstitious innovations were generally received, *etc.* Yet, truth and discipline that is seemingly new is rejected.

8. The divisions that seem to arise by it, and errors multiplying at such times. It is true, it would be a happiness if as in nature monsters (or deformed creatures) are barren, (a monster cannot beget a monster) so also this is true in spiritual things. A monstrous error could not beget another; but there must be heresies. The rending of the temple was a sign of the abolishing of that church and state, and in some way so are rents and divisions in a church. The physicians make that patient in a dangerous condition, whose distempers have an medical problem in them, that while they labor to heal one disease, they hurt another way. But still you are to know that a reformation does not make these but finds these. It is the tyranny of church officers, that make divisions in

the church, as we see by pope Victor, who excommunicated the eastern churches about a trifling business. You shall have many cry out of the diverse sects that are risen up, but yet they never blamed those that started them. I must further add its *causa, non separatio facit sehismaticum*, it is the cause, not a separation that makes schismatic. This has always been the slander cast on the Reformation, *Quot homines, tot Evangelia*, so many men, so many gospels. Luther was often required not to divide the *inconsutilis tunica*, the seamless coat of Christ. Therefore he calls his adversaries *incansutiliste, and Tunicast*. Do not lay this blame on a reformation that can only remove such things, but on those who were the fathers of these sects and schisms.

9. The ninth stop toward reform is, the outward troubles and commotions that accompany it. And certainly these lie in the way of reformation. Jesus Christ foretold, "I come to send a fire and a sword, and to set father against son, and son against father." Not that our Savior means this was the *Finis operantis*, that he intended this, but that it was *Finis operit*, there would be this event wheresoever his pure and powerful

preaching was set up. For he is not the cause of it, but the stubborn and rebellious hearts of men make it. Neither the physician nor the medicine are the cause of the pains and troubles the sick man feels, but the ill humors that have been long gathering in him.

10. The unthankfulness of people; that they should not look down upon but esteem more the priestly instruments which God sends to deliver them by. The Israelites were unthankful to Moses and Aaron. Now as this unthankfulness is a gross sin, so it ought not to be any discouragement for those who are employed in the public good. Luther was offended greatly at this, and therefore he tells us his temptation: *Cum hac itavideo, non nunquam impatientia frangor, serie cogio, nisi illa doctrina in mundu jam spara esset, me quidvis potius sacturum quam ingrato mundo ostenderem; Sed hall cogitatienes sunt carnis;* When I see this ingratitude I am sometimes broken with impatience and seriously resolve unless this doctrine had been already dispersed, I would rather have done anything then declared it to this unthankful word; but these are the thoughts of the flesh.

MOTIVES TO PURSUE REFORMATION

But yet there are many urgent motives and arguments, why reformers should go on.

1. Because God has severely punished the neglect of any order he has left with his church. Though they have done much, yet if they have not done it completely, he has been angry. Therefore you read so often, *Nevertheless the high places were not taken away.* May not the judgment on Nadab and Abihu, for offering strange fire, may not the breach of God made on Uzziah, forever awaken reformers, that they should not be conniving and indulgent to breach the least of his commands. O you worthy patriots, do not think that you are free, and at your own disposal, how much or how little is to be done for God. You are accountable to God for jots and tittles.

2. There is nothing more odious to Christ then corruptions in his church. What detestable names the Scripture puts on idols! And the false prophet is called the *tail*. When Our Savior was to purge out the corruptions from his temple, he makes a whip, and drives the polluters out. It was a strange way, but by this he would show how odious such were to him, even

as so many dogs in his presence. Consider that speech in John 4. "My Father seeketh such who worship him in spirit and in truth." God seeks such, which argues how precious and delightsome they are to him that worship him in his own way. Therefore our Savior tells the Pharisees, that, that which was highly esteemed among them as great piety and devotion, it was βδέλυγμα, an abomination before God. O! then let us not do any abominable things.

3. A third motive is, whatsoever carnal statists think, yet in doing the will of the Lord to spark reformation, we are sure of blessings. Remember those two places quoted before (for we desire they may always stick on your hearts) how ill it was when there was no law, nor no preaching priest, and then how well it was when Jehoshaphat set up those that taught the good knowledge of God. It is true, we may be a long while in the wilderness, and God for the sins of his own people may suffer the enemies to prevail, but we are always to remember the end of the Lord, mark the ends of all reformation; and you shall find them to be peace. And as we say of the sorrows and sadness of a particular godly man, it is not his godliness that makes him so,

but because he does not have enough godliness. This is the same for a church or state; it is not a reformation that makes woe and misery, but because we are *not reformed enough*, we are not willing for this.

4. Consider how much men venture to prepare ways for antichrist, and to make *his* paths straight. Do not men venture their estates, and their lives, that the man of sin may become a man of glory? And shall not we do as much for Christ? Will not the prisons and miseries in which they suffered, witness against our dastardliness? Did not the people bring their earrings to make the golden calf? Did not the Corinthians suffer the false apostles to buffet them and smite them? Shall there be martyrs for error, and not for truth? As good old Pambus wept when he saw a strumper cunningly dressing herself to please her lover, because he could not take as much pains to please God. So you should do this when you hear of the papists and Arminians and Libertines and such adversaries, making themselves poor, and venturing their lives, that error may be advanced. Why do you not humble yourself because you are not so forward, or self-denying for the truth?

USE OF EXHORTATION

We ought to prepare the way for Christ. God will reform his church by other means if we do not promote it. Take heed, lest while we are negligent, he comes down himself as it were, and scourges out all profaneness from his temple. If he would do this, you would lose both your reward and comfort. Consider that as it is your desire to prepare Christ's ways, so it is the greatest honor that God ever put on you. How many thousands that shall find the benefit and sweetness of drinking the pure streams of God's ordinances, will then bless God for you? In these matters of God do not consult with flesh and blood, and remember that he is engaged for his truth more then you. You indeed have your lives and estates to lose, but God has his honor, and his truth to lose, which is more than the entire world. How will you ever answer it if God at the Day of Judgment shall say that he put an opportunity into your hands, and you have not improved it, when the blood of other men's souls may be required at your hands? Take heed that at your death beds there is no outcry, *O my England sins!* I do not speak this in any spirit of discontent, but rather of joy, seeing those clusters of grapes you have already brought us from the land of Canaan those good and wholesome laws that have been enacted since your sitting. Only be exhorted to hold on, and take the opportunities that God puts into your hand. Those that would not gather manna in the morning, could find none all the day after: Only the man that stepped in first into the pool of Bethesda, could be healed. And you are more engaged to this by the solemn covenant you have entered into so that you must necessarily break many bonds asunder if you grow forgetful of this work. Take David for an example in the Psalms; there he had vowed to bring the ark back into a fit place. Remember how when he had in that way sworn, see how careful he was. Do you remember David and all his troubles, or more near the original way the Hebrew takes it, *in his whole affliction*, that is, *in all that trouble, and fear, and care that was upon him*, when God smote Uzziah, and so hindered him in his intended reformation? There is his grief, *where was a stop in his work*. Then consider again his resolution, he would not sleep, nor eat, (it is an hyperbolical expression of the indefatigable pains he would take) that the ark might be settled. I shall therefore pray as David, when the people were willing,

The Lord keep this always in their heart; the Lord always keep your covenant and resolutions alive in your hearts.

Now that you may not be as those who built the ark of Noah, but were drowned themselves; or a Hiram, that sent materials to build a temple to that God, who he did not know, that you may have comfort and benefit in all that is done, consider the following.

1. Humble your souls for all your failings, and sins for one miscarriage may embitter many mercies. 2 Samuel 6, When David was with great pomp and cheerfulness bringing back the ark, on a sudden God manifested his displeasure against Uzziah, not as some think, because he touched the ark, seeing he was a Levite, but because it was put on a cart whereas it ought to be carried on men's shoulders. See what a sad obstacle was put in the way. David on this leaves the ark, and will carry it no further. Take the advantage therefore on these days that all the sins which stand on your account may be wiped off.

2. Labor for a spiritual heart, to be such as can delight in the spiritual worship of God, that can account spiritual things glorious things. Men that are affected with outward glorious pomp in the service of God, it is a sign they have no spiritual things to rejoice in; the woman that has no children to play with, she can delight in dogs, and other creatures. In Haggai 2 there is a promise that God would make the glory of the second temple far above that of the former. How was this true, but because of Christ's spiritual preaching and presence there. I cannot but name a passage out of Pelusiota, (*lib.2.epist.246*), because it is so parallel with our times lately, and I wish all people were of his judgment. He says that there was one named Eusebius, a bishop, that cast out and reviled the good people, and in the meantime was very devout in building and adorning the churches. Now Isidore says the church is one thing, the place of the church another. The one consists of unblameable men, the other of wood and stone which if the bishop considered it, he would not any longer overthrow the one and adorn the other. And in the apostle's times, when the church abounded with spiritual graces and holiness of life, they had no temples. But in our time the temples are more adorned

then is fitting, but the church is scorned and mocked. If I might have my wish, I had rather be in those times in which the temples were not so beautiful, but in the splendid church, with heavenly graces, then in these times in which the temples are very glorious, but the church is empty of graces.

3. Get sincere and holy aims, even in doing God's commands; let there not be Paul's complaint, "All seek their own," and not the things of Jesus Christ. Be willing to be even an *anathema* that the church may prosper. It was a noble resolution of Tullies, *immortaliiarem quid tra rempbuclocam acciperem*, he would not have immortality itself to the prejudice of the commonwealth. You have a notable instance for this in Jehu, how did he reform according to all that was in God's heart? And yet he lost the reward; not this only, but as in Hosea 13, *God threaten to be revenged on him.* And why is all this, but because his heart was not right to God? You ought not to aim at glory and fame, but at *God's own* glory and honor.

4. Reform your own lives and conversations; for how reasonable is it that you who make laws that other do

not swear, you yourselves should not? How fit is it that you who bind others to the keeping of the Sabbath, you yourselves should sanctify it? And this again undid Jehu, that although he pulled down Baal, yet he did not reform *himself* from Jeroboam's sins. *Histeriam ne sias*, read the history of Jehu, except you yourselves be made such a history to others. O! therefore let it be true of you all, that since you have been laboring in this public reformation, you have been more holy, you have been more pure. You that have endeavored to make way for Christ in the church and state have you much more made way for him in your own family? What will it profit to have ordinances, holy worship, *etc.*, if we ourselves still remain unholy?

AN INSTRUCTION ON VERSE 2

Verse 2 is an instruction to people not to mutter under these sad calamities, if by this Christ may come and reign in his church.

Consider the following:

Gradual Reformation Intolerable

1. That a reformation does not make these troubles, but it exposes sin. Do not murmur under God's providence, as is forbidden, 2 Corinthians 10. The Jews murmured under Moses and Aaron and how many of them did God destroy? So again, the Corinthians, because Paul urged strict discipline about the incestuous person and other disorders, therefore they were prone to murmur. And so people think that this reformation is the cause of all this evil, and that reformers are the troublers of England. But it is sure that our sins and an unwillingness to be subjected to Christ works us all this woe and trouble. If we had more truth, we should have more peace.

2. How slowly we prepare and fit ourselves for mercies. It is true, speed is a great advantage in public works; the heavenly bodies convey their sweet influence, as they are swift. But yet you are to take notice of it, that our slowness in fitting ourselves for mercy is more to be blamed. It is your complaint, the parliament is slow; why not rather we reform our lives slowly, we prepare ourselves slowly, and therefore it is that good things are kept off? Moses and Aaron were not the causes that the people were kept so long in the wilderness, but

their own sins and rebellions against God were the cause. Let this therefore stop your mouths and do not discourage those who labor for your good. That is not profitable for you, as the apostle speaks in the same case.

3. How grievous a sin it is to wish for your old condition again to magnify that instead of true reform. This was the temper of the perverse and forward Jews, who wished they were in Egypt again. Moses and Aaron would destroy them for such thoughts, and see how they amplify that condition into a bondage of which they complained greatly of before! *They sat down by the fleshpots in Egypt.* The text there tells us that they "sat down" as if they had *so much ease.* And they did this by the *fleshpots,* as if they had had so much plenty. Indeed their estate was wholly different, and they were actually truly miserable. It is true, our times are very sad, and as Tully of his civil wars, so may we say of ours, *qui in hae trumpestate videre, he is not a true Christian that can be heartily merry in these days.* But were not the times of superstition, of altar worship, of silencing your ministers as bitter to you?

4. How the mercy, when it comes, will make amends for all. Canaan will satisfy for the troubles in the wilderness. That the church has brought forth a *man-child* of reformation will make all former sorrows and pangs be forgotten. When and how God will put a period to these sad distractions, we do not know; but certainly God will own his own truth, he will not forget his promises to his people. And if we should perish, yet when we have done our duty, we shall have our comfort and reward in heaven. Certainly God has not raised all these hopes of his people, to make *them more miserable*. Will God do with his people, when they have laid up all for his service, as the husbandman with his bees, when they have enriched themselves with their honey? Certainly, if the fervent prayer of one righteous man prevails much, how much rather the prayers of many thousands will prevail?

FINIS

www.ingramcontent.com/pod-product-compliance
Lightning Source LLC
Chambersburg PA
CBHW032006080426
42735CB00007B/528